W9-BZA-696

LOVE ME
NEVER
LEAVE ME

OTHER BOOKS BY MARILYN MEBERG

LOVE ME
NEVER
LEAVE ME

DISCOVERING *the* INSEPARABLE BOND
OUR HEARTS CRAVE

MARILYN MEBERG

THOMAS NELSON
Since 1798

NASHVILLE DALLAS MEXICO CITY RIO DE JANEIRO BEIJING

Published in Nashville, Tennessee, by Thomas Nelson. Thomas Nelson is a registered trademark of Thomas Nelson, Inc.

Thomas Nelson, Inc. titles may be purchased in bulk for educational, business, fundraising, or sales promotional use. For information, please e-mail SpecialMarkets@ThomasNelson.com.

Unless otherwise indicated, Scripture quotations used in this book are from the Holy Bible, New Living Translation (NLT), © 1996 by Tyndale House Publishers, Wheaton, Illinois. Used by permission.

Other Scripture quotations are taken from the following sources:

The Holy Bible, New International Version (NIV). © 1973, 1978, 1984 International Bible Society. Used by permission of Zondervan Bible Publishers.

The King James Version of the Bible (KJV).

The Living Bible (TLB), © 1971, Tyndale House Publishers, Wheaton, Illinois. Used by permission.

The Message (MSG), © 1993. Used by permission of NavPress Publishing Group.

New American Standard Bible (NASB), © 1960, 1977, 1995 by the Lockman Foundation.

New Century Version, (NCV) © 1987, 1988, 1991 by Word Publishing, a division of Thomas Nelson, Inc. All rights reserved. Used by permission.

The New King James Version (NKJV®), © 1979, 1980, 1982, Thomas Nelson, Inc., Publishers.

Names and details in some anecdotes and illustrations have been changed to protect identities or may be composites or hypothetical examples drawn from the author's personal and professional experiences.

Page Design by Casey Hooper

Library of Congress Cataloging-in-Publication Data

Meberg, Marilyn.
  Love me never leave me : discovering the inseparable bond our hearts
crave / Marilyn Meberg.
     p. cm.
  Includes bibliographical references.
  ISBN 0-8499-1951-7
  1. Loneliness--Religious aspects--Christianity. 2. Loss
(Psychology)--Religious aspects--Christianity. 3. Rejection
(Psychology)--Religious aspects--Christianity. 4. Separation
(Psychology)--Religious aspects. 5. Spirituality. I. Title.
BV4911.M43 2008
248.8'6--dc22

                                                           2007042211

Printed in the United States of America
08 09 10 11 12 QW 6 5 4 3

In memory of my thirty years of marriage to
Ken Meberg.

You loved me, but you left me. You didn't want to; I didn't want
you to. Cancer took you away. But I'll see you again in that place
where there is no leaving. So for now, you live in my forever memories.

When the time is right, babe, put the tea kettle on,
and we'll share a cup. There's lots to say and hear.

Love always . . .

CONTENTS

Introduction

THE INSEPARABLE BONDS OUR HEARTS CRAVE

O God, you are my God; I earnestly search for you.
My soul thirsts for you; my whole body longs for you
in this parched and weary land where there is no water.
—PSALM 63:1

Before we get serious about the bonds our hearts crave, are you aware of the current taste treat our society is craving? It is the humble little cupcake. Cupcake shops are springing up all over the nation. People are willing to stand in long lines just for the ultimate pleasure of a rocky road, caramel apple, butter-cream delight, or even peanut-butter-and-jelly cupcake.

This growing phenomenon has been creating a buzz, ranging from those who say the cupcake fling is a fleeting fad . . . to those who maintain a cupcake is small, gourmet, better than a candy bar and, most of all, tastes like childhood. Bingo! I'm hooked on that explanation.

How well I remember purchasing the little devil's food cupcake with a roof of white frosting from Boehm's grocery store during my childhood. It delighted my soul and was eagerly consumed in the company of one or several of my classmates on our walk home from Amboy Elementary. Not only can I revisit that glorious taste treat, I also recall what I felt as I ate it. If only for a few hours, I was distracted from the bewilderment of my math class and the fear of the teacher who found me annoyingly unteachable. That cupcake security released my fears until 10:00 the next morning, when once again, I would settle into a haze of familiar math bewilderment.

The editor of a highly sophisticated food magazine states that the cupcake's rise in popularity has to do with this nation's longing for comfort and security. Because we're living in a time of international threats, both politically and economically, people want to be transported back to a time when they and their country were innocent. I understand that possible explanation for our renewed appreciation of the simple little cupcake, but the truth is, our desire for security from a fearful environment is as old as Adam and Eve. There has never been a time when we were not fearful about something. Much as I wanted to believe my cupcake security blanket would shelter me from the math travails of the next day, reality forced me to recognize my taste treated the symptom but did not provide the cure.

The cure for Marilyn would have been a clear and competent

math mind. Unfortunately, that cure never appeared. I've given up finding it. However, I have not given up the comfort of a gooey, luscious, chocolate-fudge cupcake. You'll never convince me cupcakes will not be on the menu in heaven. Of course the heavenly element is that there will be no price to pay from calories or cavities.

I hope the book you are holding in your hands will prove to be as security-producing as a richly flavorful chocolate cupcake. There is no doubt we live in a world from which we often want to retreat and simply pretend tomorrow may allow us to pursue our innocent pleasures instead of demanding requirements beyond our capabilities. But I think it's possible to have our cupcake and eat it too. In other words, we can have security in this life and not have the foundation of that security yanked from us, as it was for me at 10:00 a.m. each day. God has clearly stated certain promises in the Bible that He means to be security producers in spite of circumstances. For example, Psalm 9:10 states, "Those who know your name trust in you, for you, O LORD, have never abandoned anyone who searches for you."

Now, I have to admit I felt totally abandoned in Mrs. Stealthway's math class. (Of course that's not her real name. She still makes me nervous, even in memory.) But feeling abandoned was simply that: a feeling. In reality, I was *not* abandoned, but reality did nothing to comfort me then. It *felt* like abandonment, and when something *feels* like abandonment . . . it must *be* abandonment (following our usual logic of, If it looks like a duck, sounds like a duck, it must be a duck). But in my child mind I hadn't a clue what the word *abandonment* meant. I only knew I felt utterly left behind, beyond rescue with no mathematically inclined duck in sight.

If I were a betting woman, I'd be willing to wager you too have experienced abandonment feelings but perhaps didn't recognize the word that labeled what you were experiencing. As a result, you may not know some of what you do, think, and feel today comes from abandonment experiences.

You may be muttering, "The last thing I could possible be feeling is abandoned. I'm married and have kids, friends, a busy job and church life. I even have neighbors . . . too many neighbors. So I can tell you for sure I do not feel abandoned. Robinson Crusoe might have been abandoned, but I'm not and never have been."

As I've been writing this book and telling a few people the topic is abandonment, the invariable question I receive is *why?* What kind of topic is that? people want to know. Are you writing for orphans or babies left on doorsteps? Are you planning on reaching only a small percentage of readers? Why don't you write about something all people struggle with, like depression, loneliness, marriage, divorce, kids, friends, parenting, jobs? You know, the usual stuff.

This book addresses all that "stuff," but I want to suggest that the greatest fear each of us on this planet struggles with is *abandonment.* It influences all the "usual-stuff" responses we have. Maybe we haven't known what to call that unexpected and sometimes overwhelming emotion we suddenly experience that makes us feel like we're hanging on to our sanity for dear life. But the fear of losing what we want and need—whether it has to do with a friend, husband, or parent—is so profound, our psyche comes up with a gazillion defenses to protect us from those uncomfortable or disturbing feelings. One of the most common ways we try to ward off the dreadful feeling of abandonment is to desperately try to control everything in our lives. You've heard of the controlling mother, wife, friend, husband, boss, daughter.

What is the need to control all about? You may be surprised to have me tell you it's about warding off the feeling of abandonment. As unlikely as this may seem to you now, I truly believe such feelings as the need to control can have an abandonment root. In this book I hope to help you trace those feelings and behaviors back to that root and then help you reprocess the event to lessen its negative impact on your life. Here's a little sample of how we'll dig out and reconsider an abandonment root. Since we're talking about the issue of a controlling personality, let's see how that behavior might come about as the "symptom" of a deeper fear of abandonment.

When we lose something or someone we want and need, we experience loss, which causes us to feel disconnected. When we lose our physical or emotional connectedness, it's like losing our anchor. (I talk about this a lot in chapter 5.) We were created for connectedness, and *dis*connectedness can create panic. We were never created for isolation. So when we lose connection, we may experience abandonment, meaning we feel on our own, not connected, with nothing and no one to hang on to.

So what do we do? We try to gain control over as many circumstances as possible. If we are in control—calling the shots—perhaps we can prevent feeling lost and abandoned. That feeling of hanging tightly to the reins of our kids, our job, our spouse, our friends—whatever—gives us a sense of security, so we control it all until something or someone breaks loose. Then the panic of abandonment occurs.

Abandonment experiences are far broader than being left on a doorstep or becoming an orphan. Abandonment feelings can come from a husband who is too busy to listen, a child who leaves home and rarely calls, a body no longer able to fight disease, dreams that do not come true, and even a God who seems not to hear. (We talk about those themes throughout the book.)

Generally this abandonment stuff plays out in ways we don't understand: in feelings and behaviors that make no sense. In my experience, for example, I've suddenly felt grief-stricken when everyone around me was laughing, though I might have been laughing myself a split-second before the grief unexpectedly enveloped me. Or I've worked much harder than necessary to prove I could accomplish something academically. I've felt lonely while surrounded by people who love me, and I've felt insecure when I've had every reason to feel confident.

When those unexpected feelings sweep through me like a tidal wave clearing the beach, I'm left standing by myself on a lonely desert island of emotions wondering, *Where did that come from? This is stupid . . . what's wrong with me?*

I believe abandonment stuff has left us all high and dry on

an occasional emotional desert island. My guess is that you too know how it feels to be dragged off into a bottomless abyss by a rip current of darkness that then hurled you back into "normal" life, where you stood on the empty beach totally exhausted and puzzled, wondering, *What was that all about?* (I describe my own unexpected empty-beach rip current in chapter 6. I never saw the rip tide coming.)

That's the thing about the way an abandonment issue can creep up on us. We don't see it rolling in. We don't know what it is, and we don't know what to do with it once it's knocked us down.

The whole issue of abandonment has to be identified and then understood. This is the good news of God-assisted enlightenment. It is possible to understand these weird and unexpected rip currents, and it's also possible to not get knocked down by them. How? By figuring out what we're feeling and then tracing those feelings back to their root. That process helps us understand why we're feeling the way we do. With that insight we can learn to manage the way we respond to those *Where-did-that-come-from?* feelings whenever they gang up like a tidal wave and threaten to wash us off the beach again.

Most of those mysterious, out-of-the-blue feelings and behaviors are rooted in fear—innate fear that the bonds holding us close to someone we love will be broken. Or we may be reacting because those bonds are already lost and our hearts feel a panicky craving to reconnect. The bottom line for us all is that we crave connection with the ones we love, and when our bond

with them is broken, damaged, or threatened, we fear being left
. . . abandoned.

I want to gently say, we've all been left, one way or another, by someone somewhere. Every one of us endures abandonment events, beginning with our birth. We lose our first close bond when we leave the womb, a place of safety and security for nine wonderful months. But after that, the lease is up, and baby is faced with unfamiliar bright lights and noise. Interestingly enough that first abandonment imprints the young soul; I loved researching the material for chapter 3. It makes more sense to me now why an infant's ejection from "womb-Eden" produces baby wails.

If you're not aware of any abandonment experiences in your life, that's probably why you're sometimes left wondering *What was that about?* when the event's residual sadness or insecurity sweeps over you at an unexpected time or place.

But here's the reassuring and exciting news I'll share with you in every page to come: even though we've all been left, and even though we all occasionally exhibit strange feelings and behaviors tracing back to that experience, there's great hope for our future. That's what I want to show you in this book. I'd like to help you identify and reprocess those feelings of being abandoned so that you're able to move on and live the life God has planned for you since the beginning of the world.

We all encounter little seepages of sorrow that can instantly hurl us back into that abyss of darkness. There are many roots of such seepages. In this book we'll follow the tracers back to some of the more common ones. It's interesting work. In fact, I've re-experienced a number of my own tracers as I've been putting this book together. I've found myself writing on a level of personal candor on topics I had not originally intended to discuss. My prayer is that you will be encouraged as you examine your own little seepages of sorrow and know we're all in it together. And I hope by the time we're finished you'll be filled with the joy and assurance of knowing you're loved and treasured by our Creator-God, who will never abandon us.

When God's Word tells us He never abandons anyone who searches for Him, we are meant to settle down and rest in that promise. Sometimes resting feels like an impossibility because our feelings can be loud and our fears overwhelming. I've written this book to provide some clarity for why we are feeling what we do. Clarity leads to light, and light leads us to the Light of the world and the God of the universe, who pushes back the darkness, restores broken lives, and ties our hearts to His with inseparable bonds of love.

That truth, sweet baby, is reason to celebrate. Now I suggest you reach for your favorite cupcake, a pot of tea, and begin your journey. God walks it with you.

Part 1

✷

LEFT CLINGING TO HOPE

one

✵

THE LOOK—AND FEEL—
OF ABANDONMENT

I have chosen you and will not throw you away.
—ISAIAH 41:9

I didn't realize my daughter, Beth, was providing a picture of what abandonment looks like when she was a nursery school dropout. I was totally mystified by her tears of protest when I left her at the Cozy School, a place warmly decorated with doggies, kittens, butterflies, and baby bears. She could play with other four-year-olds, get out of our childless neighborhood, and socialize with those far younger and cuter than I. So why was I asked to return to school and pick up my sobbing little girl who refused to be pacified by either green or orange popsicles?

Arriving in rescue mode, I bent down and enfolded her wracked little body into my arms and said, "Baby, baby, what's wrong? Why are you so sad?"

Her muffled words spoken into my neck were, "I don't want to leave you, Mama. I want to stay with you. Please don't leave me here."

So of course I took her home. We made cookies together, played Candyland, and squished Play-Doh into unrecognizable shapes. Gradually her little spirit was mollified as I promised her she would not have to return to nursery school ever again. She could go with me wherever I went and participate in all the wildly exciting duties of each day.

So Beth witnessed the complicated process of coloring my hair at Betty's Beauty for the Taking shop. She tagged along as I attended Christian Women's Club board meetings and luncheons, and she participated in the heady decisions of whether to buy hamburger or tuna at the grocery store. She had a little Barbie doll suitcase that was ready to travel with only a moment's notice. We went everywhere together. I loved it, but I didn't understand it.

Now I know what I didn't know then. Beth is adopted, and either consciously or subconsciously, all adopted kids have to deal with the idea that they were given away. Mental health professionals often describe this process as "working through abandonment issues." My precious little girl didn't understand why she couldn't bear to be left, and neither did I. But I knew without a doubt that the cruelest thing I could have done was force her to stay in nursery school.

Actually, I did have one rather vain suspicion back then about Beth's desire for constant togetherness. I flattered myself, thinking maybe she found me such a wonderful mama she simply chose me to play with instead of her fellow four-year-olds. But I now know that Beth's sobbing came from a place of anguish that was far deeper than her attachment to me. Her little heart was torn by an innate craving that neither of us could identify or understand at the time. I only knew what the craving looked like. Beth knew what it *felt* like.

All these years later, I know more about that anguish, and although it exists in different forms and plays out in different ways, I also believe that *all* of us, at various points in our lives, are affected by that dark emotion. It is a craving for an inseparable bond that will protect us from the soul's greatest fear: abandonment.

Beth is now a grown and competent young woman with two wonderful sons and a master's degree in social work. Her professional training and her personal experience have enabled her to better understand the issue of abandonment and to use that understanding as she helps others. Throughout this book, Beth will share with you some of the growth processes that are enabling her to overcome what was at one time a near-paralyzing fear. It is with enormous respect and pride that I commend her journey to you as you discover and examine how unknown, unexpected, or unrecognized issues of abandonment may have affected your own life.

I predict you will find this work in self-discovery both

troubling . . . and freeing. As Dr. Evelyn Bassoff says in her classic book *Mothers and Daughters*, "If one is to know the joy of living with abandon, perhaps one must face and overcome the terror of abandonment."[1]

THE FEAR OF GETTING LEFT

When I think of the terror of abandonment, I remember my first boyfriend, John Pitter. I used to call him Patter, or sometimes Pitter-Patter. I think I got by with that sauciness because he really respected me. I could run faster than he could; in fact, I could run faster than anyone in our school. Patter liked that in a woman. I always liked older men, and since he was eleven and I was ten, we were a good fit.

Patter dropped into my world abruptly and unexpectedly. He was, as he described himself, a foster kid. He came to live with the other foster kids living with Mrs. Selfridge, who made the best cookies in town. If I remember correctly, our town's population then was 372. Obviously, Mrs. Selfridge had lots of competition, but she always won the "best cookie in town" award at our annual school fair. I was impressed. So were the other kids lucky enough to be placed in her foster-care home. At least I thought they were lucky.

One of our favorite small-town-kid games was hide-and-seek. I found it mystifying that Patter would always tell me, "Stay with me, Ricker" when we'd all go hide. It seemed to me that one person could hide better than two, but I was flattered that he seemed to want me close by. The same "Stay with me, Ricker" was also customary for Patter to say as we walked home from school. I didn't understand that either. I was a runner, not a fighter. If he needed protection, I couldn't provide much. Besides, he was a big kid, and no one would mess with him anyway. So why did he want me to stay with him?

Mrs. Selfridge attended the church my dad pastored, and she insisted "her kids" go with her each Sunday. One day Patter told me he didn't want to hurt my feelings, but in his opinion my dad didn't "know nothin' from nothin'."

I was shocked. I asked Patter what he meant by saying such a thing. He told me that, contrary to what Dad preached, God did *not* take care of people and instead He left them whenever He felt like it. Patter's final word was, "Your dad seems nice, but he really has no idea about God, like I do. God ditches people."

Not long after this conversation, Patter disappeared as abruptly and unexpectedly as he had come. That hurt my heart enormously. Mrs. Selfridge told Dad that John Pitter had been adopted by some family "a ways away." We never had a chance to say good-bye.

I didn't know then that John Pitter-Patter suffered from abandonment issues. I didn't know then that abandonment is one of the most excruciating assaults to the psyche. I didn't know then that its resulting lacerations leave indelible imprints on the soul—tracers of feelings and behaviors leading back to early hurts and fears. I just knew he always wanted me to stay with him.

Now I know it's what we all want . . . the security of knowing those closest to us will *stay* with us.

THE DIFFERENCE BETWEEN
LOSS AND ABANDONMENT

When my grandson Ian was four years old, he was having a sandbox conversation with his friend Adam. I love sandbox conversations and eavesdropped through most of them when my kids were little. Now, as a grandma, I see no reason to change that tradition, so I lurked behind the kitchen door for better hearing.

Adam wanted to know where my husband was and why I always came alone when I visited Ian and his family.

Ian told Adam he didn't think I had a husband.

This was apparently a sobering piece of information for Adam. After a few minutes he asked how come I didn't have a husband.

Ian's response was, "I don't know for sure, but I'm pretty sure she got left."

Ian was right. I *did* get left. My husband Ken didn't choose to leave me. He didn't choose to die. Just as John Pitter-Patter had said to me, I wanted to say to Ken, "Stay with me, Meberg." But far too quickly, Ken succumbed to cancer. When he died, I felt abandoned.

No one on earth is exempt from feelings of abandonment. Sometimes those soul-lashings are less severe than others. Sometimes, with time to heal and determination to make a new beginning, those lashings don't inhibit us from moving on with life. Not only is it possible to move on with life, it's possible to experience joy and purpose in the moving. In fact, it's possible ultimately to see it working together for good.

But why is abandonment so excruciating to begin with? Isn't abandonment the same as loss? We read a lot about losses in various books and magazines. Judith Viorst's classic bestseller *Necessary Losses* discusses the inevitability of loss, its effect upon the human psyche, and how those losses play out in our interior being by dictating our external behaviors.

Most of us recognize loss but sometimes we miss—or misunderstand—the different look of abandonment. It's crucial to know the difference between loss and abandonment because abandonment is more toxic. According to the dictionary, to be *abandoned* is to be deserted or forsaken. *Loss* is defined as the harm or suffering caused by losing or being lost.

I can experience loss without anyone having intentionally *caused* it. For example, I may experience loss because of a loved one's debilitating illness or death. The loved one's death probably had nothing to do with me personally; he or she didn't *decide* to die. On the other hand, if I'm deserted or abandoned, a decision *was* made by someone to leave me. And if someone decided to leave me, my assumption is that something must be wrong with me or that something about me is simply not good enough. I must be defective, flawed, imperfect, undesirable, and not worthy to be kept.

If I am abandoned, I can assume that I am a throwaway.

Someone important to my life made that decision to throw me away. It was not a necessary loss; it was a determined event, a moment when someone rejected my very essence . . . my entire being. That is a broken bond, an excruciating rejection that produces shame. When I am abandoned, I become a shameful reject. In contrast, when I suffer loss, I may become the object of others' increased admiration and affection. Let me explain.

I've made a distinction between *loss* and *abandonment,* and I've said Ken's death was the former, not the latter. He did indeed leave and it was a horrific loss, but he did not *choose* to leave me (in spite of Ian's pronouncement that I "got left"). Why is that distinction important? Why does it matter that Ken left me through death and not choice? Because his death does not produce a sense of shame or personal rejection. In fact, there is a certain dignity to being left through death. There is no social judgment resulting from becoming a widow. I'm not viewed as a throwaway or a person unable to maintain her marriage. That respectability grants me the right to receive flowers, casseroles, cakes, and cookies after the funeral.

THE SHAME OF ABANDONMENT

Patter seemed to feel tremendous shame about being a foster kid. He never told me why he was at Mrs. Selfridge's foster home or if he had been in other homes. I knew nothing about his mother or father, and neither did I know if he knew them. His personal history was a blank page to me and possibly to himself as well. All I knew was he seemed embarrassed to be there and thought God had ditched him. Whether he knew the word or not, Pitter-Patter had been *abandoned.* Someone had chosen not to keep him.

A friend of mine was reading this chapter prior to my finishing it. When she read about Patter, she said, "I really identify with that kid. In fact, a lot of your readers will identify with him. My husband chose not to keep me, and that rejection continues to hurt as well as embarrass me. I too choose not to tell people about it. I don't lie, but neither do I talk about it if I can avoid it. Unlike widowhood, Marilyn, there's no dignity in divorce.

"No one brought flowers, casseroles, cakes, or cookies the day my divorce was finalized. That was a day most of my friends pretended to know nothing about. They too were embarrassed (embarrassed *for* me but not *by* me). They knew I wasn't the one to leave my marriage of thirty years. They knew I 'got left,' and they knew I got left because of another woman. That's not only terribly hurtful but also embarrassing because the interior tape that plays in my head is, *You weren't good enough . . . You are flawed . . . You failed . . . You've hurt your kids.* I was reared to believe divorce is a sin. If someone were to ask me what I consider to be my biggest failure, worst sin, and greatest source of shame, I'd say my divorce."

Perhaps we should pause here and do a review on shame. This is a subject that has occupied the minds and writings of mental health professionals for decades. As a result, there are many worthy books and articles that can help us understand why our shame feels so . . . well, shameful. I wrote extensively about shame in my book *The Zippered Heart,* but for our purposes here, let's simply say shame is not *what we do.* It is instead *who we perceive ourselves to be.* Shame sends messages from our very core that condemns everything about our interior being. It gnaws away at our foundational sense of worth, causing us to devalue what we think, what we feel, and who we are. When we are sufficiently shamed, we don't feel or think we are worthy to love or be loved. We believe we're worthless—worth less than nothing. Or, as Barbara Johnson used to describe the feeling, "like a zero with the rim rubbed out."

As if these deep churnings of shame aren't difficult enough, those who feel rejected often have to cope with shame's cousin, which bears a family resemblance but is born of different genes. That cousin is *guilt.*

Guilt and shame often appear to be the same, but guilt does not function the same way shame does. Guilt is connected to behavior. It springs from something we've done that we don't approve of. For example, if I behave in an unattractive manner, I will feel guilty. To relieve that guilt, I need to apologize. Once having apologized, I will no longer feel guilty.

But if I *do* continue to feel guilty in spite of apologizing and being forgiven, the emotion I'm feeling has moved beyond guilt to become shame. I am ashamed of who I perceive myself to be in addition to feeling guilt over what I did. But it's the shame that gnaws away at me, not the guilt.

For example, one afternoon when Pitter-Patter and I were

walking home from school together, he complained of being hungry. I knew that condition wouldn't last long because Mrs. Selfridge always baked cookies every day so that when her kids came home from school and entered the house their nostrils would be assailed by the smell of straight-from-the-oven cookies. That's one of the reasons I loved my "stay with me, Ricker" job. Mrs. Selfridge always invited me to have cookies along with the other kids. Those moments were as close to heaven as I ever got at 3:00 p.m. every day.

I pointed out the fact that Patter would soon have a cookie in his mouth and would no longer be hungry. Ignoring my words, he stopped dead in his tracks in front of my dad's church. "Hey, Ricker, I'll bet there's food in the kitchen there. Let's take a look."

I was horrified. "Patter, there's no food in the kitchen. That room is usually the third-grade classroom. It's only a kitchen if there's a potluck dinner or something."

"What about those communion crackers, Ricker? I love them," he answered. "They're small and crunchy. I'll bet those crackers are on a shelf in there." With that, Patter took off at a trot, heading for the side door to the church. The church was rarely locked, so I wasn't surprised to see Patter disappear into the building.

My "stay with me, Ricker" job had suddenly become complicated. I needed to be with Patter, but somehow I needed to protect my dad or God or something or someone too ill-defined to name. I sprinted to the church side door and into the kitchen-third-grade-classroom just as Patter let out a triumphant hoot of discovery.

"Here they are, Ricker, a whole box of those little crunchy crackers!" He slid down the cupboard wall, sat cross-legged on the floor, and tore open the cracker box. As he began munching, he noticed my look of horror. "Ricker, relax. These crackers aren't the body of Christ . . . they're crackers from Boehm's Grocery Store!"

I knew the origin of the crackers, but I was stumped at how to explain their symbolism and that they were more than an aisle-three item from Boehm's.

I too slid to the floor and finally joined Patter in eating a few crackers. We didn't eat the whole box; we left some for whenever the next communion service would be. But I was pretty nauseous when we exited the church side door.

That day was the first time I declined the cookie ritual at Mrs. Selfridge's. Instead I trudged home with a huge wad of guilt and shame corroding every artery in my body. I sought out my father and confessed my sin. I confessed that Patter and I had "stolen and eaten" the communion crackers, and I knew that was wrong. Dad was very kind and assured me God would forgive my sin of stealing. We prayed together, and I asked God to forgive me for not only stealing the crackers but also for giving in to Patter when I knew that wasn't right.

I thought I'd feel better after praying and confessing my wrongdoing. It had always worked before. But this time I had a persistent sense that I was bad in spite of confessing. I feared maybe I was a pagan. My understanding of pagans was that they were godless people with no religion. Our family friend Marion Bonner's only son Jessie had become a missionary to the Congo, where a lot of pagans lived. I suddenly thought maybe Jessie should have stayed home and worked with me instead.

I didn't know it then, but I was suffering from shame. I feared that somehow I had so deeply offended God that I was not worthy of forgiveness. Surely only an unworthy pagan would steal symbols of Him. And if God wouldn't, or couldn't, forgive me, then He would surely reject me. He would abandon me, and I'd get left with all the other worthless sinners who had offended Him so mightily that He cast them away from His presence, never to be allowed readmittance.

And God wouldn't be the only one who abandoned me. I was afraid if my parents really knew the pagan nature of my interior being, I'd get left—or get removed. When Patter was removed from Mrs. Selfridge's home, I figured it was only a matter of time before I would be removed from mine, especially when my parents figured out that God had ditched me too.

My fears were completely illogical, but emotions lack logic. They have no common sense! The truth is, emotions generally just sit there in a little pile of moronacy. (*Moronacy* is not a word, but I feel very strongly it should be.)

MIND-BOGGLING RESTORATION

Many years later I came to understand something about God that alleviated my fear of being ditched by Him. It came as a result of understanding Jesus's words while He hung on the cross.

To all outward appearances, in the waning hours of the crucifixion, Jesus was abandoned. His experience was so excruciating He cried out those heartrending words, "My God, my God, why have you forsaken me?" (Matthew 27:46).

Prior to the cross, Jesus endured hours of agonizing physical and emotional torture. Yet not once did He cry out. It was not until that culminating pain of separation from God that the heart of Jesus broke.

Jesus took upon Himself every sin, every pagan inclination, and all that is unholy in creation, and He died for it. Why? Because "the wages of sin is death" (Romans 6:23). For Jesus, the greatest hurt was the momentary abandonment from God, His Father. It happened because God, in His holiness, cannot look upon sin. When Jesus became the embodiment of sin, He was rejected. He was abandoned. He was ditched.

Amazing! Jesus had the same soul-lashing anguish as the boy who ended up in a foster home, the same anguish as the little girl who stole the communion crackers, the same anguish as the woman whose husband died too soon. Maybe Jesus's anguish was similar to a feeling of rejection you've experienced. Perhaps you, too, in one way or another, have felt like you "got left."

Honey, if you can identify with that feeling, you're not alone. But I've got great news for you. Jesus's separation from God—and ours—was bridged immediately the moment that sin-debt was paid. He was instantly restored to full connectedness with His Father. It's absolutely mind-boggling: we too are instantly awarded full family membership the moment we confess our sin and receive the forgiveness for which Jesus died.

That means we will *never* be abandoned by Him. We will never be a throwaway from Him. We will never be rejected by Him. We'll never be ditched by Him. We didn't get left by Him. He *chose* us. He loves us and will never leave us.

I know that now. I wish I could tell Patter.

two

☼

TRACKING TRACERS
BACK TO THEIR ROOT

Can a mother forget the infant at her breast,
walk away from the baby she bore? But even if
mothers forget, I'd never forget you—never.
ISAIAH 49:15 MSG

I have a friend, a new mom, whose fetus was pictured in his first portrait session (the prenatal sonogram) with his little arms folded behind his head, an image of contented repose. Ah, yes, the womb is a great place, providing for every possible need in the most luxurious and cushy of environments. If only we could stay there forever.

But no, we're suddenly and abruptly contractioned or yanked into a world that is no longer warm, quiet, soft, or consistently nurturing. Surely newborns wonder, *What on earth happened? Whatever it is, I'd like to go back home!*

The birthing experience is traumatizing. Not only because the baby loses comfort, but because an important bond is broken as well. He or she is no longer connected to that automatic and effortless life source that supplied all physical, emotional, and mental needs.

In this book, we're discovering and studying the inseparable bonds our hearts crave all our lives. For many of us, that craving began in a stark, traditional hospital nursery. We had lost our bond with the womb, and we wanted it back! In the womb, our mother's heartbeat constantly soothed us, and her body constantly nurtured us. There we felt completely protected, totally free from care. Life in the nursery was a harsh contrast. Dr. Alice Miller, in her book *Thou Shalt Not Be Aware*, gave voice to the abandonment she assumed newborns in traditional hospital nurseries must have felt: "The newborn infant, with his skin crying out for the ancient touch of smooth, warmth-radiating, living flesh, is wrapped in dry, lifeless cloth. He is put in a box where he is left, no matter how he weeps . . . . Eventually, a timeless lifetime later, he falls asleep exhausted."[1]

In contrast to this forlorn image is the nurturance that accompanied the births of my two grandsons, a scenario that is, thankfully, quite common today. Before the umbilical cord was even cut, each was placed on my daughter's tummy. Each experienced the trauma of womb-loss but was nevertheless assured by the familiar sound of Beth's heartbeat as well as the sound of her voice. Each of my little grandsons had to fight to fill his lungs with air, but the fight occurred in the warm, encouraging presence of the familiar life source.

We've come a long way since bleak and sterile maternity wards were considered an acceptable environment for the little terror victims. Today we realize infants need immediate human touch after birth to keep the mother-child bond intact. We've learned that the loss of the gentle motion of the womb's amniotic fluids can be somewhat replicated by the rocking chair where Mama holds her baby, skin to skin, rocking gently and buffering the newborn's arrival into what sometimes seems a hostile new world.

For many infants, that closeness continues when the new family member arrives home and is integrated into the bonds, and the routines, that hold the household together. It's common today to see parents going about their errands or activities while "wearing" an infant on their chest in some kind of sling or carrier. One mother I know claims (surely in jest) that she "wore my kids on my chest until their feet dragged the ground."

HOW BABIES LEARN TO TRUST

In contrast to today's attitude of keeping baby close, my children were born more than forty years ago, when the strongest child-rearing philosophy was "let the baby cry; it's good for lung development." Perhaps your mother, like my children's mother, thought she was doing the very best for you when she parented you this way.

Now we know better. Now we understand the soul-lashing that is inflicted when an infant is left alone to cry. Alice Miller describes how a mother might unintentionally let it happen:

At first, it is hard for her to put him down after his feeding, especially because he cries so desperately when she does. But she is convinced she must, for her mother has told her if she gives in to him now he will be spoiled and cause trouble later. She wants to do everything right; she feels for a moment that the little life she holds in her arms is more important than anything else on earth. . . .

She sighs and puts him gently in his crib. She bends to kiss the infant's silky cheek and moves toward the door as the first agonized shriek shakes his body. She hesitates, her heart pulled toward him, but resists and goes on her way. He has just been changed and fed. She is sure he does not really need anything, therefore she lets him weep until he is exhausted.[2]

I well remember the guilt I felt as my son, Jeff, was "allowed" to sob his little heart out alone in his crib. I tended to his physical needs quickly and consistently, but I dared not interfere with the process of lung development by picking him up and soothing him after those needs were met. After all, I wanted to be a good mother. And certainly I did not want to spoil him.

One day another new mother in my neighborhood was commiserating with me about her pain at letting her baby cry. She told me she would simply start the dishwasher so she couldn't hear the sounds of heartbreak coming from the next room. I tried that and found the clothes dryer was another good sound muffler.

Lord Jesus, forgive me!

The "let 'em cry" philosophy is harshly counterproductive to mental and emotional well-being because it is most often begun during those first few years of life, when trust needs to be established. Trust is one of the inseparable bonds we crave right from our first breath. We want to be able to trust that someone is there for us with love and care.

If an infant's environment is not nurturing and safe, the child does not learn to trust where she is and what is happening to her; she does not feel secure. Although she does not have words to express what she is feeling in that infant state, wordless feelings are nonetheless imprinted on the sensory network in her soul: *something is wrong; nothing feels safe.*

The Bible itself teaches us that trust in God (and, by implication, trust in our surrounding environment) is learned as a nursing infant. In Psalm 22:9, David wrote, "You brought me safely from my mother's womb and led me to trust you when I was a nursing infant."

At first reading, it may be puzzling to realize this is the same David who, a few verses earlier, questioned why God ignored his cries for help. But the fact that David complained to God, accusing Him of abandoning David when he most needed Him, is actually evidence of David's trust in his bond with God. The fact is, those who have not had the benefit of a trustworthy environment have difficulty trusting God. In fact, they have difficulty trusting anyone or anything, and typically, they withdraw into a world devoid of nurturing relationships, devoid of honest communication, devoid of meaningful contact with anyone or anything. They *want* those things, but they don't believe they're worthy of them.

In contrast, David acknowledged that he had learned to trust God as an infant, and because of that trust, he maintained close contact with God, even when life felt overwhelming and at times unsafe. He might cry out in frustration and fear, but he *did* cry out to the One he trusted to save him.

Later in Psalm 22, David wrote, "He has not ignored the suffering of the needy. He has not turned and walked away. He has listened to their cries for help" (v. 24).

At his core, David had a trusting heart.

How is such a core of trust developed? What has to happen in the life of a little person that enables him to ultimately trust himself, his environment, and God?

Trust does not come automatically. We are not born with a natural inclination to trust. It is learned. We learn it from the attitudes and behaviors of our mothers. When a mother causes her child to feel loved, valued, and cherished, the child then trusts his environment. He trusts his mother's kindness and care and subconsciously decides that he is worthy of such kindness and care.

THE MOST CRUCIAL HUMAN BOND

But when those early years of trust development are for some reason thwarted, the child experiences deep psychic pain for which at times there are no words.

I want to illustrate this kind of deep pain with a reference to what might be an unsettling source: the horrific story told in the classic movie based on Truman Capote's book *In Cold Blood,* which he described as a "nonfiction novel." Capote tells the story in first person, describing a tragic series of broken bonds and abandonments that occurred in his character's life, beginning at birth when his then-unmarried mother left him in the care of an aunt. Later, Truman did live with his mother, but the emotional hurts continued.

In the movie, his character sits in a prison cell with a convicted murderer, sharing the emotions each felt from the parental abandonment they experienced all their lives. Capote described his daily anguish as his mother would lock him in her New York hotel and go off to "do her thing" unhampered by the annoying presence of her little boy. He would cling to the doorknob, he said, sobbing hysterically, begging her to come back and take him with her. Eventually he would fall into exhausted sleep, lying on the floor by the door.

Because the book is a nonfiction novel and the movie is based on that book, I don't know if the hotel scene was fiction or fact. I do know, however, that abandonment produces that kind of despair, and Truman Capote had every human reason to despair. His remembered feelings from that hotel room sound very much like Alice Miller's assumption of an infant's feelings of abandonment in an old-fashioned maternity ward or in its new home where the let 'em cry philosophy is in play, don't they?

A lack of trust comes from such early, non-nurturing emotional environments. Instead of building trust, that kind of environment paves the path to shame, initiating the child's belief that he is not good enough, unworthy, a throwaway. And that shame envelops him in a shroud of abandonment that, unless recognized and processed, can affect him his entire life.

Mental health workers and researchers agree that the first bonding experience of a child with its mother is the most crucially important of all human bonds. If that bond isn't established, or if it is broken, the consequences can last a lifetime. Judith Viorst says in *Necessary Losses,*

> When separation imperils that early attachment, it is difficult to build confidence, to build trust, to acquire the conviction that throughout the course of our life we will find others to meet our needs. And when our first connections are unreliable or broken or impaired, we may transfer that experience, and our responses to that experience, onto what we expect from our children, our friends, our marriage partners, even our business partner.[3]

UNTANGLING THE TRACERS

Knowing that childhood pain and abandonment leave tracers that extend into our later lives helps us understand our emotional responses to life events, our hypersensitivity to current experiences. Even though we have no memory of the initial pain, our current behavior may spring from that early root. If a tracer from that root can be identified, we can learn to manage the hurt instead of being victimized by it.

Helping you discover those tracers and manage the hurt they may be causing you is one of the purposes of this book. Here's an example of how that can happen. My good friend and colleague Pat Wenger, with whom I shared a counseling practice in Southern California was, just this morning, engaged in that awful task of cleaning her garage. There was a table in her upstairs "playroom" she wanted to get rid of so—what else?—she set about finding room for it in the garage.

In the midst of her Bekins-man work, she moved a box that contained some loose photos yet to be put in an album. At the top of the stack were several pictures of Hobbes, her little dachshund who died two years ago.

Hobbes was the most ideal dog I ever met. He was adorable and loving and wanted only to please whomever he encountered. He asked for little and gave much. His beautiful brown eyes pleaded one consistent message: *Please don't leave me.* (Sweet little Hobbes had enormous abandonment issues.)

He had been picked up by an animal shelter in Laguna Beach as he wandered aimlessly down Pacific Coast Highway one afternoon. That is a highly trafficked road, so it was amazing Hobbes had managed to avoid being hit by a car. He was a thoroughly confused and utterly lost little dog who had no identifying tags. He was obviously highly bred and had been well cared for. But his origins remained a mystery as he took up residence at the shelter.

Pat "discovered" him some weeks later and took him home, where he lived the rest of his life as one who was supremely loved and never again abandoned.

Unexpectedly, as Pat came upon those pictures this morning, she sank into a heap of deep, even primal, tears. Hobbes had totally captured her heart; his presence had soothed her soul through some hard times. She had loved him dearly, and she grieved his loss. But the truth was that her tears this morning came from a deeper wellspring than the loss of a great little dog. Pat recognized a familiar feeling of "original abandonment," a wound that can bleed all over again if scratched. Sometimes the scratch comes at odd moments and for seemingly little reason. *So why this morning? Why in my messy garage?* Pat asked herself.

Together we followed a tracer back to her childhood. Pat's mother had to be hospitalized several times during the first four months of Pat's life, and Pat was sent to stay with friends of the family. Her father, though well intentioned, seemed ill equipped to take care of Pat's three-year-old brother Jerry, maintain the home, and worry about an infant. When Pat's mother came home from the hospital, she too was ill equipped to tend to her own recovery in addition to the needs of her new baby. Each time her mother had to return to the hospital, the infant Pat was tended to by new caretakers.

In addition to these separations, Pat grew up aware that her mom seemed obviously to prefer her brother Jerry. For example, Pat has a clear memory of leaning into her mother's right shoulder in church and being told to "sit up and don't lean." This was whispered while Jerry leaned into his mother's left shoulder. Pat was five, and the memory was recorded; so too was the feeling. So too were the memories of other times when her mom said, "You're too sensitive."

"You have nothing to cry about."

"Your brother wouldn't be crying like you are."

"Stop it this minute, or I'll give you something to cry about."

Pat learned that when Mom was around it was safer to have no feelings and no needs because feelings of rejection or abandonment would not be tolerated. Pat's tears were shamed into silence.

As she cried freely this morning, Pat felt that shame of "You have nothing to cry about, so stop it this minute" sweep over her yet again. The tracer for her Hobbes tears led directly back to her mother's words of condemnation about being too sensitive.

Pat knows now she is not too sensitive and that her mother's words sprang from her own rejecting and harsh mother, Pat's grandmother. Pat applies that knowledge now as a way of managing the impact of her mother's early rejection. She has come to appreciate her early experiences as a way of understanding more deeply the issues that many of her counseling clients present.

That knowledge does not change the original wound or prevent the related hurt from resurfacing. Neither does it answer the questions, *Why today? Why in my messy garage?* The reality is simply that a wound can be reopened unexpectedly. When that happens in spite of no sensible or timely reason, there's always a tracer. Following the tracer to its source helps us understand the pain, soothe the hurt, and makes the memory easier to manage.

Behaviors That Trace to Early, Unspoken Hurts

Grief isn't the only way our earliest feelings of abandonment can be transferred into our current lives. Those issues can also play out in other expressions and behaviors. Let me give you an example from my own "moving" experience.

I have the enormous honor of speaking and working for an organization called Women of Faith. Its express purpose is to palatably communicate a simple but profound message: God is crazy about you! Along with talented musicians, guest speakers, comediennes, and recording artists, we take that message "on the road" for thirty weekends a year. We travel to different cities around the country, sharing our lives and stories. I was one of the original four speakers when we started twelve years ago in churches; today these conferences occur in arenas where attendance ranges from twelve thousand to twenty-five thousand women each weekend.

Our president, Mary Graham, came on board ten years ago, bringing much-needed finesse and organization to each conference. We all marvel at her inherent sense of what works and what doesn't. We also marvel at her effortlessly warm and nurturing style of presiding over each conference. She has the ability to make each attendee feel like an invited guest in her home; that's hard to do in an arena of thousands, but every time, the women settle back, relax, and with her gentle encouragement, have a great time.

Four years ago we were flying home from a conference in Philadelphia. When we landed in Dallas, I left the others and headed for another gate for my flight home to Palm Springs, California. I was midstride when Mary called out to my retreating back, "Marilyn, if you lived here, you'd be home now."

I giggled at the Gracie Allen logic of her comment and continued on my way.

The phone was ringing as I entered my California condo several hours later. It was Mary saying she and some other friends "just happened" to find a two-bedroom apartment only an hour earlier, and it was perfect for me! "Think of the time you'll save traveling, and think how fun it will be because you'll only be five walking minutes away from us."

Almost before I knew it, I agreed and the deal was done. I moved in a month later, keeping my desert condo for those months when I wasn't traveling.

But here's the mind-boggling element in this unexpected turn of events. Mary totally organized the rental and delivery of furniture for that darling little apartment. In addition, when I walked in the door for the first time, not only was every couch, chair, and bed in place, there were green plants on the coffee table, new towels in the bathroom, and a pink-and-gold teapot in the kitchen. What more could one want? I was totally overwhelmed.

Mary had told me prior to my arrival that she had "taken care of everything," but I had no idea that "everything" extended even to dishwasher soap under the counter and English breakfast tea in the cupboard. Only Mary! Her loving and generous spirit was evidenced in every corner of my new little home away from home.

I, of course, responded in the only appropriate way one can when embraced by kindness. I cried.

(One brief but crucial aside: When I read this "Mary section" to Luci Swindoll, another core speaker for Women of Faith and my dear friend of more than thirty years, she heartily agreed with what I wrote about Mary but made this comment: "Don't you think you might mention my solitary struggle trying to hang your shower curtain and how it kept slipping through my fingers, enveloping my body and nearly smothering me in plastic at the far end of the bathtub? Don't you think you might just slip in that major sacrificial contribution I made to the move-in readiness of your little place?"

(Absolutely I need to mention that contribution, Luci! There was never a night I did not feel blessed as I pulled that curtain into position knowing it had nearly claimed your life.)

But my focus here is Mary, whose incredible generosity of spirit is a source of comfort and nurturance not only to me but to thousands of others to whom she ministers. However, that largeness of heart has come to us all at a great, though usually unheeded, price. Mary has, as we all have, unique issues of abandonment, and those issues have left tracers springing up to her determinedly nurturing spirit today.

When I asked her to describe any remembered roots that might link back to those issues, this is the story she told:

My parents had eight children. When I was ten months old, Sybil, their oldest, who was sixteen at the time, fell ill and had flulike symptoms for a couple of days. When she didn't recover quickly enough, my mother took her to the doctor, who hospitalized her.

Within a day or two, Sybil died. We don't know why. My mom thought she'd suffered enough, so she didn't want her to go through the ordeal of an autopsy. (I promise, Marilyn, that's what she said.)

When Sybil died, my mother was devastated, of course, and was very concerned about my dad; she told their nine- and eleven-year-old daughters to be sure and watch out for him. Sybil had begged to go home from the hospital, so when she died, Mother felt compelled to take her body home. It was somewhat customary in those days, I guess. Mother couldn't bear her being in the funeral home (probably because she didn't know anybody there). So they brought her body home, opened the casket, and Sybil was in the living room in her prom dress until the funeral.

We lived in a tiny frame house. Maybe that was why they thought it best to have me, the ten-month-old baby, taken somewhere else to be cared for. No one has yet remembered where I was taken or how long I stayed.

All I know is my mother never recovered from Sybil's death and throughout the rest of her life processed it extensively with me. Repeatedly Mother would look at me and ask, "Why would God take Sybil and give us you? If we were to have four girls and three boys, why did He not leave *her* instead of bringing *you*?"

I never once felt bad about the question. My heart went out to my mother in her loss, and I wondered why in the world God would do such weird and seemingly cruel things. It didn't seem fair to Mother.

My response in knowing Mary's experience and reading her words was, "Not fair to your mother? Of course it wasn't! But what about *you*? It wasn't fair to you either! What about that little ten-month-old baby Mary when no one even remembers where she went or for how long? What happened to *her*?"

Yet those questions never occurred to Mary. The needs of her mother were too pressing to consider Mary's needs. So she grew up thinking she had no needs. If any should make their unwelcome presence known, they were pushed away and deemed inappropriate, unworthy of consideration.

Today, part of Mary's lifestyle is to continue being the ever-present nurturer of others, tending to their needs however great or small they may be. Her response to those early, unspoken hurts is to constantly do for others what was not done for her.

UNINTENTIONAL ABANDONMENT

There is an important element to consider here as we discuss abandonment. Though abandonment is the result of overt choice, sometimes it is not intentional. The abandonment may have happened as a result of circumstances that at the time seemed unmanageable and overwhelming. Although the abandonment was real to the one who "got left," the intent was not to abandon him or her.

The difference is demonstrated by comparing the stories of Mary Graham and Truman Capote. Capote was abandoned intentionally. His mother chose to walk away from him. He became a throwaway.

On the other hand, Mary was not intentionally abandoned. She was literally lost in the family shuffle of confusion and grief resulting from Sybil's sudden and unexpected death. No one intentionally lost track of Mary. Nevertheless, her psyche recorded the experience and branded her soul as abandoned, leaving tracers that radiate out from that hurt place. Those tracers take the form of behaviors or thoughts that reflect the early, unspoken hurt.

The questions Mary's mother asked repeatedly—"Why

would God take Sybil and leave us with you? If we were to have four girls and three boys, why did God not leave *her* instead of bringing *you?*"—sound intentionally rejecting. But Mary's mother was a tender and generous person who had no idea how her words would imprint Mary's soul. As her mother continued to live in confusion and grief, Mary served as both witness and companion to that grief.

The way Mary's abandonment message has affected her thinking and behavior is to simply continue what she believes she does best: be a witness, a companion, and a supplier of help to those in need. There are thousands upon thousands who know and love Mary and are happy recipients of her kindness. But it is hard for Mary to receive the kindness and generosity of those many persons who love her, perhaps because the branded abandonment message is always cloaked in shame. It says, *I'm not worthy for you to do things for me, so go sit down and I'll bring you some coffee.*

To understand these feelings, as well as the totally selfless behavior that developed from the hurt-rooted tracers, Mary finds in Scripture many vivid reminders of how much she's worth to God. One of those reminders is found in Isaiah 43:3–4:

I am God, your personal God, The Holy of Israel, your Savior. I paid a huge price for you: . . . That's how much you mean to me! That's how much I love you! I'd sell off the whole world to get you back, trade the creation just for you. (MSG)

LOVED, CHOSEN, AND FOREVER SAFE

Whether they surface frequently or rarely, we all have strong feelings that impact us, causing tears to spring up unexpectedly, sending grief sweeping over us "out of nowhere," or pushing us to behave in specific ways. By studying these feelings and by following their tracers back to the events and issues that sparked them, we gain understanding that helps us cope.

As we acknowledge the damage inflicted on the crucial bonds our hearts innately crave, we also seek desperately to give meaning to our experiences, no matter how grievous the damage. The fact is, the human psyche can withstand almost any assault if we can find purpose in our lives in spite of that assault.

Our supreme purpose and meaning in life are to know, believe, and trust that we are loved by the God who does not "do" throwaways. That knowledge—understanding we are loved and valued by our Creator even more than we can comprehend—makes possible the productive lives of people like my daughter Beth and my dear friends Pat and Mary. That knowledge makes possible the productivity of all of us.

And here's the most important thing to understand: whether we are abandoned intentionally or due to uncontrollable circumstances, we are the intentional creation of the Lord Almighty. We are hidden safely in His hand because that's where He chooses for us to be, and that's where we *will* forever be.

For I am the LORD your God, who stirs up the sea, causing its waves to roar. My name is the LORD Almighty. And I have put my words in your mouth and hidden you safely within my hand. (Isaiah 51:15–16)

three

✹

THE WOMB EXPERIENCE

The LORD called me before my birth;
from within the womb he called me by name.

—ISAIAH 49:1

I'm not pregnant, Mom. There's no possible way."

My mother smiled indulgently then asked how I explained my socially questionable public vomiting in Edinburgh, Amsterdam, Heidelberg, Venice, and—most memorable of all—Paris.

I was embarrassed by my inability to "keep it down" but felt that in all probability I was simply a wimp. A problem, perhaps, with the water, the daily jostling of the tour bus, or the food. I did think it odd that I began to covet the Ritz crackers my bus companion munched on all day. I thought I'd simply developed a new passion. When we had a two-hour "browse the city" stop in Lucerne, Switzerland, I hotfooted it all over town until I found a box of Ritz crackers. I was thrilled; the Alps were even more spectacular with three or four crackers in my mouth.

Paris was indeed my city for public sharing. It was July 14, Bastille Day, and the entire population was celebrating. At 9:00 p.m. when Mom and I got off the bus tour of the Paris lights, I stepped to the curb and promptly emptied the contents of my evening dinner in the gutter. Actually it appeared to be a very patriotic observance of the day since there were several other patriots doing exactly the same thing.

As Mom and I walked the short block to the hotel, I made only one more contribution to the gutter. That did it for her. With an ill-disguised "maybe I'm going to be a grandma" twinkle in her eye, Mom made an appointment for me to see a doctor. I continued to protest, insisting I was not pregnant. (You'd think I had no knowledge about how babies came about.)

But Mom was right. I received the confirmation that I was pregnant in the office of a Parisian doctor who felt it important that I get a flight back to the States. He told my mother (she spoke French; I simply stared at the wall) he feared I could lose the baby. For that reason, he said, I should go home as soon as possible and get to bed.

I've been in bed! That's what got me in this situation, I thought in perfect English.

I took the first available flight to Los Angeles, hating to leave my mother to trudge on through Barcelona and Madrid without me. I also hated missing out on Spain. Mother was a wonderful travel companion, and this trip had been planned for a year. We both were excited to be together for three weeks as well as experience the richness of Europe.

Quite frankly, I was not only stunned by this unexpected turn of events, I was resentful. This was not the time I chose to be pregnant. A baby was on the schedule for *next* year. That was Ken's plan, and it had sounded good to me; I agreed with the plan. "How totally inconvenient," I muttered as I winged my way back to America.

The fact that I had not been able to let Ken know I'd be home in fourteen hours concerned me. (This happened long before cell phones.) He would of course be shocked by my one-week-early arrival, but he would be even more shocked when I told him why. How would he respond? I knew our budget needed my teaching income. . . . What *would* we do without that income?

Ken was indeed startled to see me walk through the door of our little apartment, and shortly he too was fretting. But in time, we adjusted to this enormous change in plans. We decided I would teach until December. The baby (Jeff) was due in February, and I would go back to teaching the following fall.

But that's not what happened.

As soon as that precious little boy was placed in my arms, my heart melted and I felt a bond unlike any I'd experienced before. When fall came, that bond had grown even stronger, and our plan that I would return to teaching fluttered away with the swirling leaves. I could not bear to have someone else mother my little boy, and Ken supported my wish to stay home with him.

I missed the classroom, yes. I had long enjoyed the intellectual challenge and stimulation of interaction with my students. But for me, at that time in my life, the right thing to do was stay home with my baby. I was fortunate that we could live on Ken's salary and our savings, and blessed that he agreed wholeheartedly with my wishes. We determined to live with less income, fewer amenities, and an unreliable car.

It wasn't easy, but I would not trade those early years for anything.

Ten years and one more baby later, I went back to teaching.

Wonderful Complexity

I learned so much as we charted little Jeff's womb development forty-three years ago. Forgive me for sounding like a reporter on the fetal-development beat, but not only is this information a fascinating confirmation of the biblical exclamation of how "wonderfully complex" we are made (see Psalm 139:14), but in this progression there is much we can learn about being loving caretakers of our unborn miracles—much of which I did not know back then.

The first dramatic motion occurring in the unborn child is its heartbeat, about three weeks after conception. This miraculously rhythmic activity continues while valves, chambers, and all other parts and connections are under construction.

Between weeks six and ten, the little body bursts into motion with graceful stretching and rotational movements of the head, arms, and legs. At ten weeks, hand-to-head, hand-to-face, and hand-to-mouth movement occurs, as well as mouth opening and closing, and swallowing. Breathing movements and jaw movements begin as well.

So much has been learned, or confirmed, in the years since my pregnancies. Perhaps you're already familiar with some of these findings, but they're simply too remarkable not to marvel over again. For example, many studies now confirm that voices reach the womb. This is amazing because the voices compete with all the background noise in the placenta. Nevertheless, baby hears Mama's voice, as well as other voices. Possibly the earliest recorded in-the-womb response to a voice is described in the first chapter of Luke.

Mary the mother of Jesus went to see her cousin Elizabeth to tell her about the divine circumstances surrounding the conception of Jesus. "She entered the house and greeted Elizabeth. At the sound of Mary's greeting, Elizabeth's child leaped within her" (vv. 40–41).

Many studies now confirm that a mother's voice is particularly powerful because it is transmitted to the womb through her own body, reaching the baby in a stronger form than outside sounds. It is wonderful these days to know so many mothers-to-be are singing to their unborn babies. Now we know how nurturing and soothing that sound is to the developing little miracle. (If you sing like I do, I can hear you saying, "Not *my* voice,

Marilyn. If I sang to my unborn baby, he probably would put his fingers in his ears or stage some other sort of prenatal protest.")

Not true. To your baby, your voice sounds heavenly, no matter what the judges on *American Idol* might say about it.

Both unborn babies and newborns seem to like music. In a study of premature infants in a hospital nursery, it was noted that infants hearing Brahms's "Lullaby" showed healthier growth and development than those little ones enduring only the non-nurturing sounds of hospital noise. It has also been reported that unborn children respond favorably to segments from Vivaldi and Mozart but react with hyperactivity to rock music. So for those of you who fear your singing would inspire prenatal protests, play Mozart or Vivaldi.

THE WOMB'S EMOTIONAL CHEMISTRY

When my children were hatching, the prevailing wisdom then (as it still is today) was to be careful what you swallowed or inhaled. No nicotine, caffeine, alcohol, or drugs. In addition, there was the encouragement to eat a healthy diet of fruits, vegetables, grains, and of course those honkin-big prenatal vitamins.

However, there is an extensive body of *new* research that can be quite sobering to the expectant mother. The research shows there is a direct chemical hookup of the mother's emotions to her unborn. Isn't that amazing?

Cell research indicates the mother's emotions such as fear, anger, love, hope (to name a few) produce chemicals that travel along the blood pathway to the placenta. Since the placenta partially envelops the baby, that means he or she may be enveloped in a chemical environment that is not always as positive as it could be. Now, obviously, it's impossible to be happy all the time while you're pregnant. As you can imagine, losing my lunch repeatedly while touring another continent did not evoke constant feelings of contentment and constant joy in me. Every mother-to-be experiences the whole gamut of emotions during those nine months when another being seems to take over her body, but judging by the overwhelming proportion of "normal" babies born each year, we must assume fetuses are tough little characters who aren't permanently impacted by occasional showers of Mom's emotional hormones. At the same time, this research encourages us to perhaps work harder during pregnancy at following Paul's advice in Philippians 4:

> Always be full of joy in the Lord. I say it again—rejoice! Let everyone see that you are considerate in all you do. . . . Don't worry about anything; instead, pray about everything. Tell God what you need, and thank him for all he has done. If you do this, you will experience God's peace, which is far more wonderful than the human mind can understand. . . . Fix your thoughts on what is true and honorable and right. Think about things that are pure and lovely and admirable. Think about things that are excellent and worthy of praise. . . . And the God of peace will be with you. (vv. 4–9)

We certainly know that emotional chemistry affects us outside the womb. How many times have people rolled their eyes at what is perceived as "unbalanced" behavior that for a woman occurs once a month? My husband not only rolled his eyes, so did I. A week later, when I "got over it" and returned to normal, I knew what had caused me to overreact to the grocery clerk who repeatedly asked for my Kroger card when I had already shown it to her and had returned it to my wallet only to be asked for it again.

And then of course we are well aware of the hormonal growth and changes that occur in the body chemistry of teenagers. We wonder if they will ever return to "normal"—and if we will survive until they do.

We could go on and on citing our behavioral responses to body chemistry that is out of balance. The reality is, we are all a walking bag of chemicals. So too are the unborn (but they swirl before they walk).

This is helpful information for expectant mothers, giving them another reason to "think about things that are excellent and worthy of praise." But it's also helpful to the rest of us adults who may be seeking the early, unremembered root of current thoughts, feelings, and behaviors that impact our lives today, perhaps in unexpected or emotionally painful ways. If we can identify a tracer from that root, we can learn to manage the hurt or the behavior instead of being victimized by it.

We generally think our feelings of being unworthy, unwanted, and unlovable are formulated in early childhood. In light of the research suggesting that some of our fears and inse-curities are with us as a result of a highly stressed womb environ-ment, it's interesting to contemplate that they may have an even earlier root. In cases where the nine months of pregnancy were characterized by consistently negative and highly charged emo-tions resulting in baby rejection, it makes sense that the little one did not get off to the best emotional start.

But does that mean the little one was born with emo-tional disabilities that can never be healed and that he or she faces a lifetime of misery? Of course not! The emotional "mood" of the womb is but one of the marvelous complexities that cause us to be who we are. In addition to emotional chemistry, many other factors are at work in the womb and throughout our lives—spiritual, physical, genetic, environ-mental, dietary, and many others—that meld us into the per-sons we become.

We're working through this book together to discover how we can live the emotionally satisfying and abundant life God created us to have, and, in this chapter, we're looking at how we might strengthen the prenatal bonds that may help launch our children into that abundant life. But by considering the effects of emotional chemistry on our children-to-be, we may also gain insight into our own prenatal experience and how it may have affected the crucial bonds that help form our psyche.

Armed with this knowledge, we're better prepared to man-age our current emotions and behaviors that may be rooted in our earliest life experiences.

REPAIRING THE RIPS IN OUR SOUL

In my therapy office some years ago, I saw a young woman who demonstrated, both in her childhood memories and in her reluctant role as a mother, how emotional chemistry before and after birth may impact behavior and feelings. Her story also shows how the emotional hurt resulting from an early abandonment can be helped once the root is acknowledged.

I'll call the young woman Cameron. She was a charming, single party-girl—and a committed pagan. She enjoyed attending law school and working part time in a law office, and when she discovered she was pregnant, she was horrified. The baby's father wanted to marry her and help rear their child, but she refused to marry him.

Her hopes of finishing law school, passing the bar exam, and ultimately establishing her own law practice suddenly seemed like an impossible dream. Never did she consider an abortion, but never did she feel any love for the life forming in her body. In fact, she felt deep resentment toward the fetus because it represented an unwanted, life-altering interruption.

She told me how much she had wished she could simply miscarry, which, in her mind, would be an honorable end to a dreaded event. Throughout the pregnancy she told herself and a few others how much she did not want the child. When the baby (Kevin) was born, he entered into a life where he was not welcomed or loved. He had been emotionally abandoned in the womb; next he was emotionally abandoned in the crib.

Kevin was a fussy baby. He arched his back away from Cameron and did not seem comforted by her efforts to feed and change him. He cried much of the time.

Then something interesting happened. Cameron told me that during one of Kevin's seemingly endless crying fits she looked at his little red and contorted face and suddenly felt sorry for him. Surprised by her own behavior, Cameron lifted Kevin out of his crib and held him close to her neck. She settled into her cozy leather study chair and began to rock him. Then she began to sing to him. She was amazed to sense Kevin settling down; he finally fell sleep.

There had been so many sleepless nights that soon Cameron too fell sleep. When she awakened an hour later, Kevin was still nestled into her neck.

That was Cameron's "aha!" moment. She started thinking about how Kevin had been calmed by her hesitant motherly gestures. She had felt there was something wrong with Kevin, but now she was starting to think differently.

She started thinking about herself and her own behavior. Why was she more comfortable with surface relationships? Why did she bolt and run whenever a man showed real interest in her and not just her fun, party-girl ways? Why had she resisted marrying Kevin's father? Why was she determined to make her own way without commitment or dependence on anyone else? Why had she moved to the West Coast to be "rid" of her parents on the East Coast?

For several weeks these questions continued to swirl around

in Cameron's mind, and in the midst of them was a stark recurring memory. She saw herself at age seven, waiting for her father to pick her up for their every-other-weekend visit at his house. More often than not, he never came.

Each time her father failed to show up, her mother would tell Cameron harshly, "*Never* trust a man, and *don't* get saddled with kids."

It had never occurred to Cameron that we often repeat the mistakes of our parents—until we learn we can make better choices than they did.

By the time Cameron came to me for therapy, Kevin was an insecure little toddler, always afraid he'd "get left." Like Beth, he was a nursery school dropout. Separating from his mother was terrifying to him. The maternal love cord he craved had not been woven for him during his womb development. The symptoms of that lack became increasingly clear to Cameron as Kevin developed frequent nightmares in which he saw himself sitting on the grass in the front yard waiting for his mother, who never came. Cameron listened and didn't need to be told how that felt.

I had the privilege of walking Cameron through her own abandonment pain, which she had experienced from her parents' divorce and from their relative indifference to her as a child. She learned how it is possible to repair rips in the soul by simply knowing where the rips are, what they look like, and, if possible, understanding why they are there. Cameron was conscientious about her repair work. She journaled, read, talked, and attempted to re-parent the little girl she had been: one abandoned by both parents and filled with toxic messages from her mother.

Then we worked on her parenting skills. With a greater understanding of the pain that can result from damage to the parent-child bond, Cameron was able to become a more sensitive and caring mother to Kevin. She ultimately married Kevin's father, and they vowed to partner in providing love and security for Kevin.

I felt hopeful, seeing the genuine desire of both parents to establish an entirely different environment for Kevin. What gave me even greater hope, however, was seeing Cameron and Kevin's father place their trust in Jesus.

Cameron is spiritually released from all that once was; she and her husband became new creatures in Christ. Cameron memorized the words of 2 Corinthians 5:17: "Those who become Christians become new persons. They are not the same anymore, for the old life is gone. A new life has begun!" When nagging messages come into her mind, Cameron recognizes the tracers and acknowledges their root. Then she quotes that verse and confidently claims her newness of life.

BIBLICAL DIRECTION, MOTHERLY ADVICE

If scientists are right that emotional chemistry affects the fetus in the womb, little Kevin didn't develop in the healthiest environment. Neither did my son Jeff forty-three years ago. Cameron's negative attitude about her pregnancy may have been absorbed, in some way, by Kevin in the womb. In a similar way, Jeff may have swirled in hormones produced by a gazillion anxious thoughts as I tried to accommodate my unexpected pregnancy. For one thing, I was instructed to stay in bed for two months after I arrived home from Paris. Apparently there was evidence Jeff could break loose from his moorings and head out too early. I did everything I was told to do so I wouldn't lose him.

By the same token, I hated staying in bed! I've never liked confinement, and the "rule" of staying put and being still was contrary to everything I wanted to do then or now. During that confinement I felt a complete loss of control over my circumstances. I had not really been consulted in all this. I thought, *Don't I have a say about something I didn't vote for? What can I do? Nothing. Just go with it, Marilyn; it's out of your hands . . . beyond your control. Whose control is it in? God's! Oh yeah, Him . . .*

In addition to those feelings, I was concerned about our finances. We needed my income. What if we couldn't make it? Our car kept lapsing into inconvenient comas in various parking lots. We also had graduate school debt and still owed my parents a thousand dollars. That loan was sacrificial on their part, but they knew we needed it to move from Washington to California. There were no strings attached to the loan, but I felt honor-bound to repay it as quickly as possible.

On top of those worries, I wondered, *How much does it cost to have a baby? Do we have enough insurance? Maybe I could skip the hospital (fret, fret).*

Like Kevin, Jeff was a fussy baby. Was it because he'd floated in a placental sea of hormonal anxiety for nine months? No one knows. Maybe he just didn't like the color we painted the nursery.

And even if the research is right and fetuses *are* bathed in emotional hormones, including those that stem from darker feelings, there's no direct correlation between crying babies and mothers who cried during pregnancy. Let's face it: Fussy babies are a part of creation. And so are "good" babies who rarely make a sound of complaint. The point is that our responsibility to our unborn miracles is to do everything we can to provide a healthy environment for them. And this research tells us that, although we live in human bodies with fret-prone brains, we need to do everything in our power to eliminate negative thinking and stress-producing experiences.

And remember, Scripture suggests we're to keep our minds on "excellent" things anyway. Plus, the apostle Paul said that we need to be content whatever our circumstances (see Philippians 4:12). (Personally, I think that's cranky advice, but of course it's true. It's just sometimes I have a hard time being content even though I'm supposed to be.)

While biblical guidance is always invaluable, I also received some very practical advice during that difficult pregnancy. It came from my mother, who suggested that instead of worrying about the future I pray for my little developing child. She reminded me that our baby had been planned by God even before He created the universe. That truth blessed me beyond measure. So I began praying for the little planned-by-God person in my womb. My spirit lifted, and my soul quieted as I did.

Of course, if I'd known then what I know now, I'd have played Mozart and Vivaldi in the background.

four

MYSTERIES OF THE MIND

I remember my affliction and my wandering,
the bitterness and the gall . . . and my soul is downcast
within me. Yet this I call to mind and therefore
I have hope: Because of the Lord's great love we are
not consumed, for his compassions never fail. They
are new every morning; great is your faithfulness.
—LAMENTATIONS 3:19—23 (NIV)

When I was nine years old my father was having some major health issues. Dad's doctor told him he needed to rest or he would die at an early age, just as his own father had died of a heart attack.

Following the doctor's orders, Dad resigned as pastor of the United Methodist Church in Amboy, Washington, and bought forty acres of utterly remote, heavily wooded and spectacularly beautiful land about ten miles from town. I stayed in the same school but was no longer within walking distance of anyone or anything except the dense undergrowth of endless forests. A gorgeous creek ran through the property, meandering its way to somewhere I could not imagine but thought I'd like to go.

It was picture-perfect property. The population of those forty acres was three: Mom, Dad, and me. (It was four if I included my dog, King.) The low population count was exactly what Dad needed. His normally gregarious and social inclinations gave way to peace, quiet, and few people. In contrast, I have never in my life not needed people, so my gregarious and social inclinations died in the breeze rustling through the evergreen trees.

Mom was teaching at the school I attended, so we drove back and forth together each day. I loved that. She was a wonderful listener and was quietly present in the midst of my emotional flailing about. Two years later Dad sold "Lonely Acres" and was appointed to the pulpit of the United Methodist Church in Manor, Washington. I loved it when we moved. I was instantly healed of all my accumulated neuroses as I rode my bike with Bev Smith, played basketball with Ed Charter, and listened to the love life of Ina Chapin. Who could ask for more?

Because Ken had heard the good, the bad, and the ugly about Lonely Acres, he wanted to see the place. It was a major side trip on our way to Seattle one summer day in June, early in our marriage, but we swung off the I-5 and headed for Amboy and Lonely Acres.

I had not seen the property in fourteen years, so as we traveled up Bosewell Road I felt warmly nostalgic. After all, there were good memories associated with Lonely Acres too. As we topped the hill at the end of Williams Road, we were enveloped by a dense undergrowth of trees nearly shrouding from view the little valley below. We got out of the car and looked down that long, winding road that dropped down into the valley where my former house was located near the meandering creek.

Suddenly I felt faint—nauseous and terrified. Nothing looked quite the same, but for some reason it *felt* the same.

Ken rushed over and helped me sit down. "What is it? What's wrong? You're shaking and pale. Marilyn, are you sick?"

I didn't have a clue what was wrong, but I had a sudden memory of standing in that very spot as a ten-year-old kid scanning the long driveway down to Williams Road waiting for my parents to come home. It was five o'clock. They were supposed to be home by four. Had they been killed? Was I now an orphan? Who would take care of me? We had no neighbors . . . no phone . . . I was the only child in the universe.

Reliving that forgotten memory, I was once again terrified. I threw up in the grass—in the very spot where I had thrown up fourteen years earlier. Fourteen years earlier, King had comforted me. Now, as I relived my terror, it was Ken who did the comforting.

In reliving that memory, I remembered then the rest of the experience. About 5:15 my parents came tearing down Williams Road and topped the hill to find me sitting nonchalantly on the grass, waiting for them as if nothing were wrong. As I crawled into the car for the short trip down to the house, both parents apologized for being late, explaining that Mom had an unexpected faculty meeting that delayed her (and of course that was before cell phones).

I told them, "No problem. King and I just decided to walk up to wait for you." I never told them I'd been so terrified I'd thrown up and had tried to figure out how I'd live in an orphanage where, like Oliver Twist, I would need to beg for more gruel.

I didn't know it then, but I had been feeling the terror of abandonment. Fourteen years later, I felt it again. The memory had not been summoned; it just came crashing through to my conscious mind.

The Unbidden Release of Buried Memories

What is often confusing about those images that suddenly reemerge is that they can seem unrelated to what is happening at the moment. But they are triggered by something in the environment that causes the unconscious to release the buried memory. There is always a purpose in that release, and that purpose is related to our ultimate healing from the hurt associated with that remembered experience. More about that later.

My daughter, Beth, had a similar experience when she too unintentionally relived an abandonment memory; hers was rooted in the very first hour of her time on earth. Beth was a young adult when she began her search for her birth parents. When she found them, she learned that they had been high school sweethearts when her birth mother, Sherry, became pregnant. They were too young to marry, and abortion was out of the question. But being an unwed mother was scandalous, so Sherry's parents sent her from the Midwest to the West Coast to give birth.

Later Sherry and Steve married and reared a family together, never telling their children, their friends, or the members of the church Steve pastored about the baby they had given up for adoption. When Beth learned their identities and nervously made that life-changing phone call to them, all of that changed. They quickly welcomed her into their family back in the Midwest and later introduced her to their church.

Shortly after Beth and Sherry became acquainted, they went together to the facility in Los Angeles where Sherry had stayed during her teenage pregnancy and where she gave birth to Beth. Just as I was terrified by a forgotten memory when Ken and I revisited Lonely Acres, Beth was similarly affected when an abandonment memory came crashing down on her there.

I've asked Beth to share a portion of that experience with you:

When my birth mother, Sherry, came to California to visit me, we visited the maternity home where she had stayed for the two weeks prior to my birth. During this visit I discovered that when Sherry had been there, twenty-three years prior, the facility also had an attached hospital where the girls would go to give birth. During our tour we took the elevator down to what used to be the hospital, just as Sherry had done in the early morning hours of August 16, 1967.

As we came out of the elevator and were walking down a corridor, I experienced a wave of strong emotions. I became dizzy and lightheaded and had to stop to get my balance. Surprisingly, the emotions I felt were terror and despair; tears sprang up in my eyes. The woman from the maternity home who was giving us the tour noticed I was crying. When I shared what I was experiencing, she told me we were in the corridor I had been wheeled down in an Isolette immediately after birth. I was taken to the nursery where I stayed until going to a foster home to await my adoption.

A second experience of remembering happened a few years ago during a professional training session dealing with trauma. The participants were asked to pair up and practice some therapeutic interventions to help process our own traumas.

During my turn at being the client, I chose to deal with a car accident I had been in on Valentine's Day, which also happened to be the day my husband had asked me for a separation. While describing the picture of me sitting on the curb with the other driver after the accident, both of us unharmed and waiting for the police to arrive, the picture changed.

Suddenly I saw myself curled up in the fetal position on the cold, hard sidewalk. As I continued to describe what I was experiencing, it was clear that my mind was taking me back to the Isolette in that maternity home in LA.

I felt cold, alone, curled up, and utterly abandoned. Again tears sprang to my eyes. My chest felt tight, and my head was swimming with emotions—terror and despair that I did not want to relive at that moment.

Wanting it to stop, I was, with the help of the trainer, able to visualize Jesus picking me up off the sidewalk and rocking me in His arms, comforting me and restoring my peace.

For many years I had sensed that dark memories rooted in my earliest moments of life were locked away inside of me. But I avoided fully processing those early memories. They were too scary, too raw. They made me feel so vulnerable and alone. They filled me with the fear that I was not lovable and no one wanted me.

It is no wonder that, thinking back to that Valentine's Day when my husband asked for a separation, I was so quickly transported to my first feelings of abandonment. Not having been held by my birth mother as a newborn but rather having been whisked away to an Isolette had left a wound that did not heal.

A growing pool of research surrounding pre- and post-birth experiences, indicates that babies can have emotions and memories rooted in their earliest moments that profoundly affect their feelings about themselves and their place in the world. Based on my own experiences and my own professional studies, I firmly believe this is true.

But I also learned, through my own experiences and professional experiences, that healing of those profoundly hurtful memories can occur. After the trauma workshop, I went back and did some good therapeutic work with that same trainer.

That work helped me reprocess those early memories and remember something else: that I was never alone. Jesus has been with me all along and will never leave me or abandon me.

One might expect that Beth's visit to the place where Sherry had stayed and where Beth was born might provoke emotions—but the nondescript hospital corridor? The unexpected image that flashed to Beth's consciousness was of those moments when she had been in that corridor before, and the image unleashed the emotions she had felt when she was there as a newborn. Those feelings had been stored in her memory bank. When they pushed their way to her conscious mind, they were so overwhelming Beth had a strong physical response—dizziness—and an emotional response—tears. Beth pulled herself together to continue with the tour, but afterward she thought, *What was that about?*

Now she knows what she didn't know then.

THE MIND'S MYSTERIOUS STORAGE SYSTEM

Now, please forgive me for interrupting our discussion, but if you've read any of my books you know I occasionally lapse into foolishness and insist upon taking a little giggle break. And since we're talking about the crazy way our minds work, it seems appropriate to throw out a bit of crazy silliness now. So, with apologies to all blonde women, I have to share this joke with you that gives me a giggle.

A blonde woman was speeding down the road in her little red sports car and was pulled over by a woman police officer who was also a blonde.

The blonde cop asked to see the blonde's driver's license. She dug through her purse and was becoming progressively more agitated.

"What does it look like?" she finally asked.

The police woman replied, "It's square, and it has your picture on it."

The driver finally found a square mirror in her purse, looked at it for a moment, and then handed it to the policewoman. "Here it is," she said.

The blonde officer stared into the mirror, handed it back, and said, "Okay, you can go. I didn't realize you were a cop."

Isn't the mind a marvelous thing? And one of the most amazing things about it, at least in my experience, is that it can suddenly go AWOL without any indication that it was even considering an extracurricular excursion. I love that joke because I frequently have moments when I identify with those two blondes as I sigh to myself, *Marilyn, where is your mind?* The answer is on the corner of my desk where a teacup coaster reads, "My mind not only wanders, it sometimes leaves completely."

In this chapter we're considering the power of abandonment memories to suddenly come crashing down on us in unexpected ways, provoking unexpected physical and emotional responses. But where, exactly, do those memories come crashing down *from?*

Memories are hidden somewhere within the mind, which, as we've just discussed, sometimes has a tendency to play tricks on us. The mind is a part of the brain, which, fortunately, is trapped inside our skull so it can't slip off with our mind when it goes tiptoeing through the tulips in la-la land. There's no easy distinction to be made between the mind and the brain, so I won't try to define one except to say the brain is utterly fascinating and far too complex for my mind to grasp. Research tells us the brain consists of around one hundred billion nerve cells (neurons) that send and receive signals, as well as nearly five thousand billion helper cells that support the activity and survival of the neurons. Somewhere in all that mysterious maze of cell business is my memory. (I knew it had to be somewhere.)

To many of us, memory can be frustrating, because it too tends to go missing occasionally or (in my case) frequently: "I think I remember buying her a birthday present, but I can't for the life of me remember where I put it. On the other hand, do I really remember buying her a present, or did we just have lunch instead? Now that I bring up the subject, where did we have lunch if indeed we did, and what did I order?"

Even though specific memories are sometimes hard to summon forth when we need them, our memories are never banished. They remain in the brain's "memory vault," waiting to be summoned—or perhaps hiding when they *are* summoned.

The mystery and wonder of the mind and its system of storage is another tribute to the God who created us all, as the psalm says, in that "wonderfully complex" fashion.

Reprocessing Abandonment Memories

Researchers who study memory have yet to fully comprehend its miraculous intricacy. With that in mind, I don't want to reduce the mystery of memory into "Dick and Jane" language. But for the sake of simplicity, I'd like to suggest we see ourselves as little walking, talking photo albums, and that we switch from the metaphor of the memory vault to the memory album.

We go about our lives carrying troubling pictures we don't know we have—or if we do know we have them, we'd like to throw them away. But since memory doesn't throw *anything* away, we try to forget the troublesome photos. When that happens, the images get pushed down into the unconscious, where the album is protected and safe.

But the fact that those pictures are in the album and that we sometimes receive flashes of them tells us we need to look at them, exclaim over them, and perhaps cry over them. When we acknowledge the hurt, pain, confusion, or embarrassment they may produce, our next step is to show them to the Father who, incidentally, already sees them, and then to ask His help in processing them.

It may also be helpful for us to seek out a trained professional who can help us feel safe as we learn and feel the contents of our albums. After experiencing the Lonely Acres flashback with Ken, I put it back in the album—not to be forgotten but with no clue what it meant or how it influenced my behavior. It slipped into the pages of my conscious-mind album under the heading *What was that about?* Later I had a trained professional help me page through my memory album so I could reprocess that abandonment memory, incorporate Jesus into the revised version, and make it easier to live with.

It is incredibly comforting to know God is not indifferent to my lifetime of *What's that about?* experiences. But notice that *He* doesn't ask the question. *I* do. Sometimes I get an answer, and sometimes I simply must rest in what He knows and I may never know. I trust that He has a plan for my life (see Jeremiah 29:11) and that He knows what He's doing. As the Old Testament character Job humbly said to God (after enduring some harsh setbacks and asking *What was that about?*), "I'm convinced: You can do anything and everything. Nothing and no one can upset your plans" (Job 42:2 MSG).

REPROCESSING MEMORIES YOU DIDN'T KNOW YOU HAD

Beth didn't know she had felt abandoned so early in life . . . until the scene flashed before her in the hospital corridor. As a newborn she had seen it and felt it, but then her brain tucked the memory away into her memory vault. Thirty-five years later it reemerged in a strong way, and she sought out professional help with processing it. With the aid of that empathic professional, Beth reprocessed that memory to eliminate—or at least reduce—its hurtful impact.

With the psychotherapy trainer providing a safe, reassuring

environment for her to relive the memory, Beth saw herself in all her helplessness and vulnerability as she was rolled away from her first mother in the cold and non-nurturing Isolette. She was heading into nine days of having her needs attended to by a competent but overworked staff in an environment completely unlike the warmth and safety of the womb she had so recently left behind.

Instead of seeing herself alone in the nursery, attended to but not loved, Beth saw Jesus smiling over her Isolette. She saw him as described in Zephaniah 3:17: "He will take great delight in you, he will quiet you with his love, he will rejoice over you with singing" (NIV).

Abandonment memories can be harsh and hurtful. But the pain they inflict is soothed when we see, instead, the Creator of the world *singing* over us and taking great delight in us. There is great relief in seeing ourselves held in His arms, our faces nestled into His neck.

The ultimate solution for both the question and the pain of abandonment is found in God's promise to always be with us. Of those many promises, here's my favorite. If you've seen my hair, you'll know why this one speaks especially to me.

> I created you and have cared for you since before you were born. I will be your God throughout your life-time—until your hair is white with age. I made you, and I will care for you. I will carry you along and save you. (Isaiah 46:3–4)

five

OUR INTENSE NEED FOR CONNECTION

*If we walk in the light, God himself
being the light, we also experience
a shared life with one another.*

—I JOHN 1:7 MSG

I have one incessant need: to know how, why, or who started what—the origin of things. All things capture my attention. I suppose that's one reason the study of psychology has always fascinated me; it deals with origins and behavior that spring from those origins.

When a mother bends down to envelop her sobbing little child and asks, "What's wrong, baby? Why are you crying?" what is it Mother wants to know? She wants to know the source, the cause, the origin of her child's tears. And why does she want to know? So she can understand where the pain came from and how it got its start. In the mother's effort to know who, what, or why her child is crying, she forms a method, not only of how to comfort, but also how to explain and hopefully eliminate her child's hurt.

For example, I was six years old when my family moved from California to Washington State, where my father became pastor of the United Methodist Church in Amboy. The two-room school was within walking distance from the parsonage where we lived. It was a frightening school to me because grades one through three were in one room and grades four through six were in another. As a first-grader, I felt everyone else was older, wiser, and bigger than I. There was one boy, John, who felt unusually frightening to me; he knew it and capitalized on it. Although he too was six, he ate too many Twinkies and Hostess cupcakes to be anything but bigger than anyone in what was designated "the little room."

Every morning as I walked to school, carefully picking my way around the endless rain puddles, John would lurk about the puddles waiting for me. Then he'd dash over to a puddle and slam his fat foot into its center, creating a tsunami-like splash that totally drenched me. Every morning I would gratify his need to bully by crying helplessly, turning and walking home to change into dry clothes.

One morning my father was home to witness my humiliation and tears. As my mother sorted out some dry clothes for me, Daddy said, "How long has this been going on, Marilyn?"

We had moved to Amboy only two weeks earlier; since then

it had been "going on" daily. When Dad learned this, he asked me through my tears, "Marilyn, why are you putting up with John's splashing?"

His question stunned me into silence and stopped my tears. "What am I supposed to do?" I answered. "He's mean, he's fat, and he hates me!"

"None of that matters, Marilyn," Dad said. "He's a bully, and I'm going to teach you how to handle a bully." My peace-loving mother sighed and left the room. My feisty father sprang into teaching mode.

Now here's what was happening: Dad was first seeking to know why I was crying. He wanted to know the origin of my tears. Then he sought to explain a method that could eliminate my future tears, which would hopefully enable me to cope with a bully.

Looking back, I know now what I didn't know then: the origin of my tears was deeper than the bullying behavior that triggered them. Their origin was the helpless fear I had that I wasn't cut out to "do" school.

The school year had started three weeks before we moved to Amboy, so I felt everyone else already knew how to read, spell, and figure out arithmetic before I arrived. And of course many of the kids *did* know more than I did because some of the students in my room were in the second and third grade. In addition to all that was the sure knowledge that Mrs. Smiley (who didn't) was close to detesting me. I felt enveloped by a hostile environment where I was the outsider who would never fit in and would never learn to read, write, or do math. (I still don't know how to do math, but I did learn to read and write.)

On top of all that fear and inadequacy was my immediate hatred of the relentless and incessant rain. The question continually in my mind was, *Why did we have to move to this awful place, and why do I have to go to a school where I'm hated?* I felt utterly rejected and alone. John's daily splashing only underscored my perception of myself. I was helpless, pitiful, and abandoned by the entire universe.

But then my father entered my dreary world of thinking and feeling, bringing with him a solution. He taught me how to do the one-two punch. "Make a fist," he instructed. "Now punch me in the stomach. Then when I'm bent over in pain, my head lowered, come up under my lowered chin and punch again!"

We practiced until he thought I got it and he could no longer stand the punches. Then he drove me to school and apologized to Mrs. Smiley for my tardiness, saying he didn't think it would happen again.

The next morning I once again was picking my way around the puddles on my way to school. John was lurking as usual. But this time instead of him coming toward me with an upraised foot, I dashed toward him with an upraised fist. I punched him in the stomach. When he doubled over in pain, his chin was lowered and I punched it too. I had just performed the perfect one-two punch!

John fell back into the puddle originally meant for me. I stood over him in triumph and warned him to never, *ever* splash me again. Crying and soaked, he slunk home to change into dry clothes. He never bothered me again. In fact, he never came near me again.

Now, I am not advocating fighting as a remedy for helplessness, fear, or abandonment. But I *am* recommending that you choose to take action in the face of these feelings rather than continuing to feel victimized by the situation. The first action step is to identify the origin of our distress. The next step is to become empowered to change it.

My father traced the origin of my tears and helped me feel empowered instead of like a victim. I was overwhelmed by what appeared to me to be insurmountable circumstances. The one-two punch empowered me to claim my rightful place in the universe, which had previously felt hostile and rejecting. Somehow, when I exhibited strength, my universe became more user friendly: John didn't splash me, Mrs. Smiley complimented me on my developing reading skills, and even the rain gave way to an occasional ray of sunshine.

Now, as I look back, and especially as I watch my grandchildren, I question the wisdom of using the one-two punch. After all, not all recipients of the punch would have gone slinking home. The whole puddle scene could have escalated into full-scale war with the new kid from California becoming the target of other six-year-old warriors. My mother certainly wanted empowerment for me but would never have recommended the one-two punch.

Though this discussion never occurred, I'm guessing my

mother would have preferred that I use some sort of diplomacy with John. I could perform unexpected and kind deeds for him, which might startle him into more civilized behavior. She would have encouraged me to talk to him before he splashed me and try to find common ground, like our mutual passion for the chocolate cupcakes with vanilla rooftops. She probably felt that, were I patient, in time, John would find me boring and find some other victim. In the meantime, I would have continued to be a soaking-wet little saint in anticipation of John's better side surfacing.

At any rate, my point here is that there's always an origin for our tears, and to the degree it's possible, I want to understand it, fix it, and move on. I want to know why we do what we do.

WHY ARE YOU CRYING?

So how do we respond when we ask ourselves, or someone else asks us, "What's wrong, baby? Why are you crying?"

Sometimes I may cry because my chemistry is out of whack. Maybe I need blood tests to see if I have an overactive or underactive something or other. Maybe I'm just hungry; that's an origin easily discovered: *Mercy, Marilyn! The last time you ate was forty-five minutes ago. No wonder you're cranky. You need chocolate!* Or maybe I'm tired: *You need more sleep, Marilyn. You've stayed up reading until 1:00 a.m. four nights in a row. Turn your lamp off earlier and see if you don't feel better the next day. Or find a dull book. That's another solution. You never read until 1:00 a.m. out of duty.*

Tracing the origin of our behavior and figuring out the

possible reason for what we said, did, or felt is helpful to us as it can motivate us to make a few changes. For example, when we moved to the country outside of Amboy, I felt completely disconnected. To be disconnected is to face isolation with no feeling of being tethered to anyone or anything. That disconnection is stressful and usually distressing because the psyche requires connection at almost any cost.

Connection to what? Connection to people. A tethering that means we have relationships, which cause us to feel a sense of place, a sense of belonging, and a sense of mattering to someone.

Back in the early days of the space program, astronauts who had to leave the space shuttle and "work outside" had to have a tether that connected them to the spaceship.

Imagine how it would feel to be one of those astronauts, completely dependent on that tether. What if some malfunction caused it to break? The astronaut might be lost in space; floating off helplessly with no hope of retethering and no hope of ever reconnecting with the mother ship, colleagues, family, friends, or the earth.

It is not an exaggeration to say the fear the astronaut would have experienced at being disconnected from the spaceship is what all of us feel when we experience emotional disconnection. Our emotional need of connection is as great as the astronaut's need for connection to the spaceship. When abandonment occurs, the tether disappears, and we float about, lost in space. We feel panic and fear that cause us to scramble wildly to reconnect; we are desperate to reestablish and secure our tether.

That disconnection is one of the origins of the newborn infant's frantic crying. The loss of the womb with all its security-producing amenities creates a nameless panic. One of the solutions to quelling the panic is for Mama to hold the baby close to the familiar sound of her heartbeat and the warmth of her encircling arms. There are, of course, other possible causes for baby's tears (including being wet, hungry, or ill), but the origin of those first tears is the disconnect from Mama's womb.

NEUROSES CAUSED BY DISCONNECTION

My family's move made me feel disconnected from society, and at the risk of sending you into a mild coma over yet another Amboy story, I want to illustrate how my disconnection at Lonely Acres affected my health and sense of well-being.

One of my more noticeable and peculiar neuroses was the fear that I would throw up whatever I ate. At first, I was careful about what I ate because I thought it might prove especially challenging to my digestive system. So I avoided Almond Joy candy bars, cookies, cake, pie, or any other sweet thing that would now inspire in me a bare-knee crawl to reach and devour.

But my fear of throwing up my food became more complicated with the passing of time. I soon limited my food intake to simple things like bread and milk . . . maybe a soft-boiled egg, but nothing complex like broccoli or steak. This peculiar behavior alarmed my parents enormously. I was losing weight as well as stamina.

The behavior became even more peculiar as I formed a mild panic if I didn't have a bucket by my bed at night. The purpose of the bucket was the security of knowing it was right there if I woke up suddenly and couldn't get to the bathroom on time.

Coupled with that behavior was the before-bed ritual of having my parents listen to everything I had eaten that day and assure me there was nothing I'd consumed that could produce vomiting. I became uneasy if either of them seemed impatient with my food recital. It scared me that their distraction might cause them to miss a food culprit that could then be responsible for my needing my bucket.

Poor little Marilyn. My heart goes out to that anguished nine-year-old kid who felt so isolated and alone she developed a huge neurosis to protect as well as distract herself from the source of her behavior: feeling totally and utterly disconnected from the world.

A neurosis is a functional disorder of the mind or emotions without an obvious organic root. That disorder produces anxiety and possibly phobias. My phobia about eating had its root in anxiety. I felt anxious about having lost connection with my social world. My parents were a connection. Books were a connection. My dog, King, was a connection, but I needed more. I needed other kids, several grocery stores (at least), and a year-round school where I could compete to be named fastest runner of Amboy Elementary and slowest thinker in math. I needed to go into a restaurant and see people I'd never laid eyes on before.

I needed to see how they held their forks and used a napkin, and if they made mouth noises.

And still, thousands of years later, I dislike isolated places. I want people action. I don't have to necessarily interact with them all the time, but I want them around me. If for any reason I should be forced to live on a far-away-from-it-all property, the first thing I'd buy before I left civilization is a bucket. Sooner or later I'd probably need it. (Interestingly enough, I never once threw up during my mild insanity at Lonely Acres; therefore, I never used my security bucket.)

Certainly I cannot build a case that assumes anyone going to a remote property will experience the sense of disconnection and isolation I felt. I can, however, build a case that unmet emotional needs—such as our need of connection—can be toxic for us all and can show themselves in unexpected times and ways. Fortunately, just as hunger tells us we're not getting the food we need, neuroses or emotional outbursts or other odd behaviors are often warning signs that we are not getting all the emotional food we need. I had a basic need to be connected, and my neurosis was making sure I recognized that this area of myself was starving.

Why do I have such a fierce need to be connected to others? The answer to that question is simple: God did it. He created us for connection, which develops then into relationship. His original design for His creation was that we have unending connection and relationship with our Designer. Divinely placed in the very core of each human soul is an intense need for connection. We express that connectedness to God through prayer, our thought life, and our behaviors. We express that connection to each other in the same way. We don't pray to other people, but we care about them and express that care with our words and behaviors.

That connectedness builds relationships, which sustain us by the nurturing presence that comes as we interact with each other. Galatians 6:2 encourages our connectedness: "Share each other's troubles and problems." As we connect and share each other's insecurities, fears, or inadequacies, we are reminded in Psalm 68:19 that our Creator does the same for us: "Praise the Lord; praise God our savior! For each day he carries us in his arms."

The image of being carried daily in the arms of God, next to His heart that beats out an unending rhythm of love and connectedness, is overwhelming in its promise of nurturance. Being held in the arms of our mother next to her beating heart of love and connection has its root in the reality of God's consistent expression of love for us His children.

So there you have it. God placed in us the need to connect, and my own childish, irrational behaviors were trying to tell me that I wasn't getting enough of it.

six

LEFT BY DEATH

Now you are sad, but I will see you again and you will be happy, and no one will take away your joy.

I love the spunky humor for which Winston Churchill was known. When asked for a comment about death, he said that people make too much of it. He went on to say that not only do people make too much of it, so too do all religions. But after thinking a second, he added that he might possibly alter his views in the near future.

Death is impossible to ignore, and perhaps if it is reduced to some kind of witticism, it's easier to talk about. A late-night television comedian quoted someone as saying death is something that comes along like a gas bill one can't pay. The doctor, concerned about being politically correct, might say death is a "negative patient outcome."

However we describe death and to whatever degree we allow it to creep into our consciousness, it is an inevitable experience for all of us. That being said, the death of those we love produces a profound sense of abandonment. It is the ultimate of all disconnectedness, which is why we want to skirt its inevitability whenever possible. The finality of that abandonment can overwhelm the senses.

When Ken was diagnosed with pancreatic cancer, he frequently used humor to soften the gut-wrenching reality of that news. I must admit I too was often relieved of my pain as Ken frequently turned the inevitability of his death into occasional bursts of humor. My all-time favorite story of how Ken relieved tension for us both during that fourteen-month illness is one I've told before. But with your kind indulgence, I want to share it with you again.

I must first give you a bit of my hair history so this story makes sense. My hair became noticeably gray by the time I was sixteen. I started to color it at age twenty-seven. By age forty, I wondered if I should just show my age and not color it anymore, thinking that possibly being forty warranted gray hair. I asked Ken for his opinion. He strongly encouraged me to continue coloring. At age forty-five, I consulted him again about this issue, and he continued to have the same strong response.

However, when I hit fifty, it seemed to me that some sort of half-century commemoration was in order. I thought I should let my hair grow out. Also, I had become increasingly concerned about the widely published carcinogen potential in hair color. Ken adamantly maintained I did not need to go public with my hair.

A couple of weeks before Ken died, I sat down next to him and told him I needed to discuss a weighty issue. He became very solicitous, thinking I had finally decided to talk about business stuff—like insurance forms and paying the mortgage. In other words, practical realities. (Such topics tended to put me in a mild coma no matter what the circumstances.) The conversation went something like this:

"Babe, you know you're going to be leaving me soon."

"Yes."

"Well, I really need to talk to you about my hair."

"Your hair?"

"Yes, my hair. You know, there really is no point in my continuing to color it if you're not here. I think I'll just let it go."

"You're serious, aren't you, Marilyn? I can't believe it. You really are going to do it; I can tell."

He looked at me for a few long seconds, and then, with that familiar twinkle, he said, "Okay, you go ahead with that plan, but I'd like to suggest you do it in a way that will give you mileage."

"Mileage? Mileage for what?"

"Now, bear with me. How long do you figure it will take to grow out?"

"I have no idea. I don't know what's under there."

"Well, okay, let's assume three months. Here's how you'll get mileage. After I'm gone, don't go out. Don't go anywhere until your hair has grown out. When it's out, you go out."

"Babe, I'm sorry, but I don't get it. How on earth do I get mileage out of that plan?"

"Think about it. You'll probably be totally white-headed. No one will have seen you since the funeral. When you appear in public with white hair, everyone will be overcome with compassion for you. They'll say things like, 'Have you seen Marilyn? Oh, bless her heart. She's turned totally white since Ken died. They were so close, you know.' People will take you to dinner or the movies or both. You should be able to work that one at least a year."

One of Ken's most endearing qualities was his wonderful sense of humor. I laughed as Ken laid out his plan for my hair, and I laugh still. Who but Ken Meberg would come up with a scheme to ensure an occasional meal for his white-haired widow?

FACING DEATH HEAD-ON

I have always felt humor and laughter are a great way to mitigate pain. That's why my first book was entitled *Choosing the Amusing*. But I also believe we must not use humor and laughter as a way of denying the circumstances that cause our pain. When the cause of our pain is death, we need to face that experience head-on. I thought I had. What I had not faced or even knew I would need to face was the overwhelming feeling of disconnectedness and abandonment when Ken died. That was no laughing matter.

Ken was always a planner. He thought through and planned for every possible situation. He would have loved the writing of Malcolm Gladwell and his well-received books *The Tipping Point* and *Blink: The Power of Thinking Without Thinking*. Gladwell talks about how people make instinctive decisions based on conditions where there is great uncertainty. Ken and I knew he was going to die, but we were uncertain about when that event would occur. Faced with that uncertainty, we made some instinctive decisions.

Knowing he had been given four to six months to live after diagnosis, Ken immediately planned a Caribbean cruise for us and our then-still-unmarried kids, Jeff and Beth. We had a blast. We snorkeled and hiked (when we got off the ship), and we ate, slept, and laughed.

One of Ken's favorite pranks was to cut in the food lines so he could be first to be served. He got by with it because he'd tell the waiting people he had cancer and was due to die sooner or later. He had lost so much weight he did truly look as if it could be "sooner." People caught on to his black humor and affable manner; he soon became a ship favorite.

One of those "blink" decisions for me was to put the people in my counseling practice on hold. I did not want to miss any of Ken's living moments. I also promised him he would not die in a hospital. If at all possible, he would, when the time came, never have to leave the familiarity of our bed. With the help of hospice, I was able to keep that promise. I've never regretted that instinctive decision to simply not leave him until he left me.

Getting left is the common theme that accompanies death. It's an unavoidable truth as well as an unavoidable feeling. Beth movingly expressed those feelings at Ken's funeral service. With her permission, I want to share with you what she said that day:

There is no possible way for me to stand here and tell you, in a nutshell, what my dad meant to me, so I won't even try. But I do want to share with you a promise I made to him that I was able to keep and a gift he gave to me that I will always treasure.

When I was a little girl, I used to sit on Dad's lap and he would ask me to promise him that I would never leave Daddy. Every time, I would, with the utmost sincerity, make him this promise. I even went so far as to say I would nurse him when he got old and sick. This was a game that went on through all my growing-up years until I wrote him a poem one year for Father's Day when I was seventeen:

> I said I'd never leave you,
> But, Dad, I was very young.
> I'm having second thoughts now,
> Oh, maybe I'm jumping the gun.
>
> I just wanted to warn you,
> That there could come a day,

That I would go back on my word,
And I would go away.

But I will always love you.
My dad you will always be.
So if that day does come,
Please forgive me.

I thought at that age this would be a natural course that life would take. I didn't think in a million years that I would really be able to say, "Daddy, I never left you."

Dad stirred up a strong desire in me to be with him as much as I could his last year. His knowledge impressed me, and I tried to soak in his wisdom. His enthusiasm for the little things in life excited me. He was always exuberant at Christmastime about the gifts he was giving. He was so creative and never ceased to amaze me.

This last Christmas, Dad gave me a gift I will always cherish. He gave me a rocking chair. He bought it unfinished and finished it himself and carved my name and the year on the back. I know in the years to come I will sit in that chair and think about Dad, and someday I will rock his grandchildren in that chair. What a great gift!

People at a time like this often want to know if I have any regrets. The only regret I have is that when I was a little girl I didn't make Daddy promise that he would never leave me.

FEEL IT TO HEAL IT

After Ken's service, I went back to work immediately. I'd felt bad to have basically abandoned the people with whom I was counseling and felt I owed them my immediate presence. For three weeks I listened diligently and counseled compassionately. Those clients were dear people who had momentarily asked me to walk their walk with them as they worked through some issues in their lives.

But by the fourth week after returning to my practice, I was having trouble concentrating on their words and tracking with them through the events they described. It was almost as if I were in the next room, unable to hear or see clearly. It wasn't that I ceased to care; I ceased to be there. There was, in essence, no one sitting in my chair. It seemed so unfair to them for me to again say I was needing another break. But I had no choice. I could hardly charge them money to sit in a room with only my shoes, pants, and blouse in the room.

We were . . . I was living in Laguna Beach, California, at the time. Walking that beach had always been a favorite activity for both of us. The ocean sounds and smells never fail to be therapeutic for me whatever the time or occasion. During this time, I spent hours walking the beach, or sitting on the bench looking out over the little village in exactly the same spot Ken and I used to sit in anticipation of baby Jeff's birth. It was all so familiar. It was all so agonizing.

You may have heard the pithy little phrase "You have to feel it to heal it." I have to say that simple phrase is profoundly true. Though the words *cancer* and *death* were totally unfamiliar to me when they first crashed into my world, I had fourteen months to accommodate them. Gradually they worked their way into my frame of reference, and I thought I was keeping up. When Ken quietly went into eternity at 6:45 a.m. on May 5, 1990, with Beth on one side of him and me on the other, it was a sweet moment. He was out of pain. He was able to talk again and laugh again. I was flooded with peace. *Thank You, Jesus,* I breathed. *He is Your child . . . You have carried him home.*

I had grieved his diagnosis. I had grieved his gradual decent into the ravages of the disease. I thought I had grieved fully and deeply. But I had not. I didn't know I had not until late one afternoon when, after an hour's walk, I sank down into the sand to watch the perpetual drama of the ocean.

Suddenly I was tossed back on a memory wave some forty-two years earlier to Lonely Acres. I was sitting in the grass again with my dog King, waiting for my parents and terrified they would not come home. Sitting there in the sand, this time with my cocker spaniel Ashley, I was overwhelmed with the feeling Ken was not coming home . . . not ever. As the onslaught of those feelings threatened to drown me right there in the sand, I became a child again, tragically wondering, *Who's going to take care of me?*

Years earlier, I couldn't imagine being left an orphan in Lonely Acres, and forty-two years later, I could not imagine being left a widow in Laguna Beach. I had known and loved Ken since I was nineteen years old. He was not only a fantastic companion and the father of my children, he took care of me.

I felt alone, disconnected, and utterly abandoned. The desperation of my feelings poured out with such racking sobs I shocked myself as well as Ashley. I had not noticed that my sweet pet had crawled into the well of my lap and was licking my tears away as fast as she could. She so wanted to soothe and comfort me . . . make the pain go away and the tears stop. But that was not her job. It was mine. I truly had to feel it to heal it.

Just exactly what does that mean, and how does "feeling it" help heal the disconnect that comes with abandonment?

To feel my pain so intensely was to also release the buildup of energy that had accumulated over those fourteen months. I had no idea I would feel so lost. That fact was made clear to me as I cried so uncontrollably on the beach. I needed to understand that my pain meant giving myself loving permission to take some time off from meeting the needs of others. I needed some time alone. I needed to journal my thoughts and feelings. I needed to nestle in the support of a few select friends who harbored me no matter where my feelings took me or even how I expressed them.

My feelings, no longer contained but openly expressed and released, allowed me then to heal. That took time. Each of us has a different timetable for healing, and it is crucial we kindly allow ourselves to heal without someone telling us, "You should be feeling better by now."

They don't know. You do.

THE PROCESS OF LETTING GO . . .
AND MAINTAINING A CONNECTION

So then, how do we deal with an excruciating sense of disconnectedness and abandonment? I had to first acknowledge that I felt overwhelmingly lost in my disconnectedness. When I was stopped in my tracks and unable to function, I realized loving care was in order, and I had to actively grieve. But there have been and continue to be ways I maintain my connection to Ken. The primary way is in my memory. I remember the crazy hair story, the years of laughter, the meals at Victor Hugo Restaurant on the bluffs of Laguna Beach, our unbelievably bad wedding pictures, and our equally bad honeymoon in a rainy place in Oregon. The list in my head goes on. I draw it forward whenever I feel the need of connection.

For Beth, one of her major connectors was the rocking chair Ken gave her on our last Christmas together. She truly did rock Ken's grandchildren in that chair, and now, with the passing of time, she rocks herself. Jeff refuses to give away Ken's Pendleton shirts, which are too small for Jeff but are still a touch of Dad in the closet.

The words of Daniel 11:32 have inspired me for years: "The people who know their God will display strength and take action" (NASB). When Ken died I couldn't stand in strength until I first stumbled in weakness. It was only then, after I acknowledged and allowed my weakness, expressed it, and with time, stood firm in the God of the universe, that I was enabled to take action. What kind of action? For one thing, I had to learn to pay the bills, understand the mess of income tax, and cope with the inflexibility of the word *mortgage* and those in charge of it. I also had to learn that one of life's hardest realities is letting go. In the words of Emily Dickinson:

> This is the Hour of Lead—
> Remembered, if outlived,
> As Freezing persons recollect the Snow—
> First—Chill—then Stupor—then the letting go.

The process of letting go and moving on is basically the same for all relationships, whether we're letting go of a spouse, children, parents, or friends. We acknowledge the great pain of disconnect and trace it back to its origin. Then we "display strength and take action." Ironically, in working through the process, there is the promise of joy in spite of the pain. That promise connects us to Jesus, who said,

> These things I have spoken to you so that My joy may be in you, and that your joy may be made full. . . . Your grief will be turned into joy. . . . No one will take your joy away from you. . . . Ask and you will receive, so that your joy may be made full. . . . These things I speak in the world so that they may have My joy made full in themselves. (John 15:11; 16:20, 22, 24; 17:13 NASB)

seven

WHEN KIDS CLIMB
THE FENCE

And I am sure that God, who began the good work
within you, will continue his work until it is finally
finished on that day when Christ Jesus comes back again.
— PHILIPPIANS 1:6

I was four years old, walking along the edge of a very busy highway. I did not know the highway, and I had no idea where I was going. I did know my name was Marilyn Ricker, that I lived in Gridley, California, and that I was walking alone. No one knew where I was; no one saw me leave. The feeling I had was one of exhilaration; I felt powerfully in charge of my universe.

My feeling of euphoria was short-lived as a black Chevrolet ducked out of traffic and screeched to a stop on the side of the boulevard where I was conducting my victory march. I stopped.

The car quickly backed up, and then a man got out of the car and walked toward me. I knew the man. It was my father. He did not look pleased. Undaunted, I said in my most charming voice, "Hi, Daddy. What are you doing here?" I believe our pleasantries ended there.

What had possessed me to unexpectedly climb a fence and walk out of the security of my backyard? I had stuff to play with there, including a swing that allowed me breathtaking views of the neighborhood. I had not been mistreated and was given a decent and I'm sure nutritious breakfast prior to my decision to "walk."

What possessed Christopher Columbus to head out on repeated journeys into the unknown? He didn't just take off once. He took off over and over again only to die in obscurity. The fact to be remembered about Columbus was that he made what perhaps were the most significant voyages in recorded history and forever changed the world. Had I known his name and contributions, I could have used him, during my roadside conversation with Daddy, as an example of one who also had an itch to explore beyond the fence.

Now, I of course did not show wisdom when I expected to be "let go" at the age of four. My parents' concern for my safety and well-being was legitimate, and any sensible parents would do what mine did in spite of Christopher Columbus. But what motivated me at an inappropriate age was a desire to experience new things, see new things, and feel new things. Those very motivations scare parents, understandably so. Our kids can show a lack of maturity, which results in poor judgment and with that, hurtful consequences. So how do we know when to tighten the leash and when to let it drop out of our hands?

To begin with, we parents need to take refuge in the fact that not one of us is capable of parenting perfectly. It is not in us. We were born from imperfection, and we pass on the imperfection. Who do we blame for our imperfection, our inability to be perfect parents who will produce perfect children? It's that couple who had a short stint with perfection but thought better of it and chowed down on the forbidden fruit.

They so tick me off.

THE LEASH WE WANT—BUT STRAIN AGAINST

If you're inclined to expect more of yourself than is possible, may I encourage you not to be too hard on yourself? Lighten up. Here's the good news. We can choose light rather than dark and in so doing allow the light of Almighty God to give us wisdom that does not come naturally. In other words, we aren't alone. God won't leave us on a dark path; He promises to shed light on that path.

We also need to remember that, more often than not, it's natural for persons to jump the fence to see what's on the other side. Parents must not personalize that natural curiosity and assume there must be something wrong in the home of the kid from Gridley that caused her to hotfoot it down a foreign thoroughfare. So then, let's talk about "how tight the leash." In so doing, I'd like to suggest that those of us who hang on to the leash most tightly are those who most fear loss. Remember, loss leads to disconnectedness, which is basically abandonment.

It is an interesting paradox of human nature to realize we all want a leash—and at the same time strain against it. We long for the freedom to jump the fence but will ultimately panic if we don't remember where the fence is and how to get back to it. (On my Gridley walk, I had not been free long enough to panic, but that would have happened eventually.)

We see this push-pull with the little child learning to walk. There have never been words to describe what that sense of freedom and independence means to the budding little walker, but the face shouts the words. It's the look of total exhilaration at being free of constraint, whether it's the arms of those who wish her safety or the playpen that assures imprisonment as well as safety. The child learning to walk is over the moon. Mother's milk has been fantastic, but baby's own feet and legs put milk in the shade.

Those moments of independent mobility are Thank-You-Jesus moments that would be accompanied by the "Hallelujah Chorus" sung by toddlers all over the world. Even so, the little choir members want to make sure Mama's in the audience, listening and watching.

DROPPING THE LEASH

As children grow and develop into "their own person," the wisdom of a too-tight leash comes into the arena of family debate.

When they are little and dependent and lack wisdom, the leash is there for protection, but when he's just turned eighteen, is it time to drop the leash? Is there then a limit to parental protection that must be handed over to the kid you still remember looking back at you for assurance as his unsteady legs enabled him to lurch about the house?

The drop-leash moment for me came soon after Jeff's eighteenth birthday. He and his friend Jay wanted to drive into Los Angeles to the Forum for an Aerosmith concert. To say I did not have peace about that outing is putting it mildly. What about the forty-five-minute drive on the crazy Los Angeles freeways with weird people on them? There was no other way to get to the Forum, so what about that? And then there's the atmosphere of a rock concert—what about that? Would there be a haze of marijuana smoke hanging over the place, and would most of the people be drunk?

"Mercy! Are you out of your mind in even asking?" I muttered for several hours.

With the leash tightly clenched in my unyielding right hand, Ken led me into the family room and became Jeff's lawyer. That "in-chambers" session went something like this:

"Marilyn, Jeff has had his driver's license for two years. He has continually proven his competence and dependability as a good driver. I know he won't be hot-dogging his way about the freeways. (Visions of early lurchings came to mind, but I said nothing.) And in addition to that, Marilyn, Jeff has that dependability gene we saw in him early in life. Remember when Jeff was only four years old and your mother asked him to be in charge of reminding you, Marilyn, to return those books you borrowed from her at Christmas? In fact, we have all counted on Jeff to remember and follow through on the tasks we've piled on him. He has always done the dependable thing."

"Okay, babe, I know that's true, but he's never been in a rock concert environment before, and what if his better instincts and training desert him and he's caught up in all I've tried to protect him from?" (I was the zealous mother who monitored television and movies as to whether or not they were acceptable to "our standards.")

"Marilyn, it's time for Jeff to determine his own standards. You have done your part. Now it's up to him. You are going to need to sit back, let go, and cheerfully tell him to have a good time."

Around 1:45 a.m. I was in bed, staring at the ceiling while trying to remember Scripture verses to the steady backdrop of Ken's untroubled snoring, when I heard the key in the front door. Jeff stealthily walked into the room, leaned his six-foot-five-inch frame against the doorjamb, and whispered, "I'm home, Mom. And I'm the same unpolluted boy you sent out into the world of drugs, alcohol, and weird drivers. You can go to sleep now. I really love you."

"I love you too, baby. I have complete confidence in you."

I heard him smile in the dark. We were still connected.

It was time for Jeff to climb the fence and take a peek at what lay beyond. He was too old for me to chase down in a black Chevrolet. But he came back; he has always come back. Incidentally, I lost his leash. I think it found its way under the couch in the family room only to be dragged out years later by Ashley. It made a great chew toy.

AGREEING TO DISAGREE

Not only did I learn I must drop the leash and let Jeff leave as he needed to, but I also had to drop the leash in my desire to control the thinking of my adult children. Sometimes when they think differently than I do, it can feel like a disconnect to me. I wonder, *Where did they get* that *idea? They certainly did not get it here in this house. Why, for goodness' sake, those ideas don't fit the room.*

Ken and I were staunch Republicans. We cared about social issues but thought people needed to stand up for themselves and work toward establishing their personal dignity by not depending indefinitely on welfare programs. Jeff tends to share our political leanings, but Beth has always been what her brother describes a "bleeding-heart Democrat." She was a rescuer as a child, and she continues to rescue as an adult. She feels strongly that people of faith have an even greater responsibility to care for those who cannot care for themselves. (I can't disagree with that.) As a social worker she is able to campaign for those causes about which she feels strongly.

These differences of opinion have made for lively discussions as my two adult children heatedly debate their differing points of view. I stand back in admiration as I listen to Beth express her views, but at the same time, in the core of my being, I want her to think more like I think. Why? Her views feel like a disconnect to all that we used to be. Apparently, that feels a bit threatening to me. Is it not safer to agree? Doesn't agreement mean harmony and at the same time give me confidence that the mental leash has not been yanked out of my hands?

I've come to realize that the greatest respect I can show, not only to Beth, but to anyone with whom I may be in disagreement, is to agree to disagree. And in so doing, I preserve the dignity and right of all persons to be who they are and how they have come to believe. (As a total non sequitur to the topic, I'd like to say the organized church needs to lighten up, love more, criticize less. There are so many ungodly splits in the church based on judgmental mind-sets you'd think Jesus never said we were to love one another. Mercy! Don't get started, Marilyn!)

LETTING A CHILD GO . . . TO FIND HER OTHER FAMILY

The greatest challenge I've experienced in my need to let the kids go has been with Beth's search for her biological parents. It has at times felt like an excruciating disconnect for me. I've written about the experience in other volumes, but for this book, I'd like to give you Beth's perspective. She feared not only abandonment from me if she began her search but also abandonment from "the people" she might find. She knew she might find them only to have them reject her.

Interestingly, throughout the process, she too had times of experiencing a disconnect, but those feelings came neither from me nor from her biological family. She expressed the disconnect with a question: "How do you connect with people when you've been chosen and everyone else is born? It's this lack of connection and feelings of being different that persist for me, which at times make me feel like an outsider."

This past Christmas, while Beth's boys were in California for several weeks with their father, she flew to Dallas, where just the two of us spent a week together. We talked, we ate, we saw several movies, and we cried a few times. The tears came as we talked about what abandonment feels like, how it looks to others, and more specifically, how it has felt to her. No matter how many times we've talked through the years, there is always some new little tender place we manage to find in each other that needs a soft touch only we can provide.

I asked Beth if she would write some of her thoughts and memories of her adoption experience for me to use in this book. That's why you'll find bits and pieces of her writings scattered about as you read. But I specifically wanted her to write for you her perspective on how she felt and what she thought as the "search-and-find" process was set in motion. Here's what she wrote:

Finding my birth parents, Steve and Sherry Boothe, unzipped a part of my heart I didn't even know existed. There were emotions and fears that had been securely tucked away that all of a sudden were exposed. I feared I would be disloyal to my adoptive family by searching. I feared my biological family would reject me. Yet I had an overwhelming desire to be known biologically. It was not possible to be known in that way before. It was a strongly felt need.

Fears of being disloyal were magnified, given the timing of my search-and-find work. Dad had died only six months before I found the Boothes. However, not knowing how long the search would take and having heard stories of searches taking years, I never anticipated that the search consultant I had hired would find them so quickly.

It's typical that initially a search is focused on finding a birth mother, and from there, an adoptee can choose to pursue finding the birth father and possibly other biological family members. But I found the whole package at once. The reality that my birth parents had gone on to marry two years after I was born and were still married with three children was miraculous on the one hand and overwhelming on the other. The discovery added to my feelings of disloyalty. I had a dad, and he had just died. Finding my biological father seemed to dishonor Dad's memory.

What comforted me through my struggles with these feelings of being disloyal were Mom's encouragements and support and the reminder that Dad had given me the adoption papers that had been the catalyst for my search. It was Mom I first told after the search consultant called to tell me she had found my biological parents. It was Mom I cried with as I made my plan to call them the next day. And it was Mom who helped facilitate my very first meeting with the Boothes.

That first meeting took place in Kansas City, where the Mebergs gathered for our first Christmas without Dad. Dad's sister, my Aunt Marge, and her family lived in Kansas City, and ironically the Boothes had also made plans to visit dear friends there during the week between Christmas and New Year's. Given this sentimental time of year, being with Dad's family magnified my feelings of disloyalty. However, the coincidence of the Boothes, living in Illinois, and me, living in California, having both made plans, prior to my finding them, to be in Kansas City for the holidays, was too much to ignore.

Again, Mom's reminder that God knew, before the foundations of the world, that I would be reunited with my biological family, helped calm my fear. It was Mom who drove me to the hotel where I met the Boothes for the first time. It was Mom who understood and honored my desire to meet them by myself. It was Mom who helped explain the importance of my search and my find to the rest of the Meberg family, who were struggling with their own grief at the loss of my dad and I'm sure questioned the timing and wisdom of this first-time meeting with my birth parents.

Though I did find my biological father, this has not diminished my love and honor of the father who raised me. Dad died when I was twenty-two years old. He was diagnosed with pancreatic cancer during my final semester of college. I remember his desire to live long enough to see me graduate from college. He wanted to see me launched. God granted him this desire.

God also granted me the privilege of witnessing Dad's launch into heaven. I was by Dad's bedside when he died a year after my graduation. I had slept by his bedside for two weeks prior to his death to give Mom the opportunity for some sleep so she was able to take care of him during the day. Mom and I worked together to provide Dad the dignity he deserved during his last days. Mom and I were together with Dad when he took his last earthly breath. I describe this experience of being with Dad when he died as a privilege because I believe death is a sacred experience.

Finding my birth mother was also a sacred experience. It was a rebirth. It was a transition in my life that has taken me to a different place emotionally and to a new understanding of who I am. Yet, in anticipation of this experience, a fear of rejection emerged from a place in my heart I hadn't known existed. I feared that my birth mother, having moved on with her life, would find my resurfacing an unwelcome disruption. I imagined that my existence was a well-kept secret that she would not want exposed. I feared that my searching would cause her pain and in turn would cause rejection for me.

The morning after I received the names and phone number of my birth parents, I woke up with my eyes swollen shut by hives. My fear of rejection had emerged in physical form. Pushing aside my hesitation, and glad I wasn't going to be knocking

at their door that day (given that hives are not my best look), I called the number given to me by the search consultant.

When a woman answered the phone, I paused, terrified. I could hear through the phone a lot of noise in the background, so I asked, "Is this a good time to talk about something important?"

She said yes but asked that I wait while she switched phones. The wait felt like an eternity, but when she came back on the line I took a deep breath and said, "My name is Beth Meberg, and I'm an adoptee in search of my birth mother. If you are Cheryl Boothe, I think I have found her."

After confirming my birth date, I heard the most wonderful words ever said to me: "We have been hoping and praying for this day for twenty-three years."

The affirming truth that my birth parents had never emotionally abandoned me was overwhelming. My fear of rejection was wiped away, and in its place was the hope of being known in a way I had never experienced before.

My birth mom, Sherry, and I talked for over two hours. She shared with me that she and my birth father, Steve, had met when they were both twelve years old in junior high. Steve had led Sherry to Christ, and they had fallen in love with each other. As their relationship grew, their physical relationship progressed as well. When they found out they were pregnant, their plan was to marry and live in an apartment upstairs from Sherry's grandmother. Upon telling their parents, this plan was vetoed and a very different plan began to formulate.

I would be "put up" for adoption. Life then would go on as if nothing had happened. But something did happen.

Today I am growing, not only in the understanding that something happened, but in realizing who I am in that happening. I am understanding that I am not a random event that surprised God. Instead I am one for whom God had a plan. He continues to work that plan for my emotional and spiritual good. As Mom would say, "I like that about Him."

Beth did not climb the fence to look, see, and feel new things. Instead she walked through the gate. What sobers me is knowing that gate had been ordered up by God. He knew what I did not know. There were things Beth needed to see, feel, and experience that had nothing to do with me. They had everything to do with the sovereign working out of His plan.

The working out of God's sovereign plan is not always a happy experience, so I need to take a minute here and say a word to those of you who, like Beth, have conducted your own search-and-find mission for your biological mother but, unlike Beth, have been tremendously disappointed and hurt by what you've discovered. Perhaps your biological mother was indifferent, disinterested, or totally rejecting of you. Sadly, that is a far more common outcome of the search-and-find experience than the words Beth heard: "We have been hoping and praying for this day. . . ."

Anguishing though it is, a negative response to your search does not mean God's sovereign plan is not accomplished. The

God of the universe planned for you, lovingly superintended the reason for your birth, and tenderly watches over you. You are His child. As Beth has learned, you are not a random event thrust into an indifferent world with no purpose or anchor. Your purpose is to respond to the love of your heavenly Father, who never has and never will abandon you.

So, with that word of encouragement, let's go back to our thoughts about being a parent and knowing when we need to drop the leash. Remember the verse, Philippians 1:6, printed at the beginning of this chapter. You and I must remember that it is God who "began the good work" in us and in our children. It is God who "will continue his work until it is finally finished."

When will the plan be finished? When Jesus returns. Or, if we beat Him to the punch, in eternity.

So then, if we, His beloved creation, can swallow down that truth, we can drop the leash and let the kids leave when the time comes, knowing that just because *we* let them go does not mean God does. We can relax. Someone smarter than we are holds on to us and our kids forever. That means we never lose connection with Him.

We are never abandoned.

eight

You'll Know When the Time Comes

There is a time for everything. . . .
Now is "THE ACCEPTABLE TIME."
—Ecclesiastes 3:1 nlt, 2 Corinthians 6:2 nasb

Back in the days when I used to actually do more than *dust* my kitchen, I was one of those uninspired cooks who wanted a specific recipe for everything. I hated it when someone told me, "Just add a little turmeric to your cacciatore, and you'll be amazed at the delicious difference."

"How much is *a little?*" I always wanted to know. And I didn't want to hear that it was somewhere between a pinch and a dash. I wanted a specific measurement.

The same was true when it came to baking. Recipes that said

"bake until browned" sent me pacing the kitchen floor, constantly opening the oven door and fretting over whether the pie crust was actually brown or merely tinted tan. What I wanted to know was exactly *when* the pie crust needed to come out of the oven.

Many of us mothers want the same kind of directions when it comes to dropping the leash and sending our kids out of the kitchen, where they may have been securely tied to our apron string. Phrases like "You'll know when the time comes," or "Time will tell," or "Give it a little time," or "Wait and see" send us into panic or depression or both. The entity of time in those phrases is too ill-defined, almost mysterious and elusive.

Hearing those statements, we may ask, "But how do I know for *sure* when it's time?" When we receive the ambiguous, "You'll just know when the time is right," those of us who require definition and specifics become frustrated. We'd prefer the 2 Corinthians 6:2 recipe because it involves no guesswork. It's a flat-out statement: the acceptable time is *now*.

Okay then . . . that feels better.

Those who need to know the time is exactly now are also those who need a meat thermometer. They don't want to leave anything to chance. That prime rib was too expensive for some sort of airy-fairy cook-float around the oven.

Yet most of life defies the specifics of a meat thermometer. That's why phrases like "You'll know when the time comes" originated. The phrase throws the decision back to us and our knowing; it involves events that can't be poked with a meat thermometer so we're assured, "Now is the time."

In this book we're looking at those inseparable emotional bonds our hearts crave, and we've seen that the bond between child and mother is crucial to the child's well-being. Now we come to the inevitable question: When is an acceptable time to *leave* Mother?

Surely all of us agree that mother-leaving has to happen. But how do we, as mothers, prepare our children for and support them through that leaving without making them feel we're abandoning them?

And, looking at the event from the adult children's perspective, if and when they leave, how responsible are they for our possible feelings of abandonment? To what degree do our ex-children need to protect us from feeling disconnected as they go off into the wide world? How can we help them avoid feelings of guilt that make them decide to forgo their trip into the wide world and remain behind the fence, knowing that if they stay, we can at least see them, know where they are, and not feel the loss of them? Is it best for Mom to not have a "now is the time" moment?

RECOGNIZING THE MOMENT IN LIGHT OF OUR CALL

There comes a stage in all of our lives when we ask ourselves those questions—either as mothers or as adult children who begin to feel strong fence-climbing urges. As mothers, we want to do the right thing for our kids at exactly the right time. And as kids, wanting to be good *ex*-kids but also wanting to demonstrate love

to our mothers, we may long for the meat thermometer that says exactly when it's time for mother-leaving.

I believe it helps us sort out these questions if we remember that each of us has a calling, an innate, individual purpose for our lives that may be different from anyone else's call. With that in mind, let me ask you a seemingly unrelated and perhaps startling question.

Do you think Jesus abandoned His mother?

Two scriptural references suggest that possibility. The first time occurred when Jesus was twelve years old. We read about it in the second chapter of Luke. I'm going to quote the passage here so you won't have to look it up.

> Every year Jesus' parents went to Jerusalem for the Passover festival. When Jesus was twelve years old, they attended the festival as usual. After the celebration was over, they started home to Nazareth, but Jesus stayed behind in Jerusalem. His parents didn't miss him at first, because they assumed he was with friends among the other travelers. But when he didn't show up that evening, they started to look for him among their relatives and friends.
>
> When they couldn't find him, they went back to Jerusalem to search for him there.
>
> Three days later they finally discovered him. He was in the Temple, sitting among the religious teachers, discussing deep questions with them. And all who

heard him were amazed at his understanding and his answers.

His parents didn't know what to think. "Son!" his mother said to him. "Why have you done this to us? Your father and I have been frantic, searching for you everywhere."

"But why did you need to search?" he asked. "You should have known that I would be in my Father's house."

But they didn't understand what he meant.

Then he returned to Nazareth with them and was obedient to them; and his mother stored all these things in her heart. (vv. 41–51)

What a fascinating glimpse into the mother-son relationship between Jesus and Mary. At first, Jesus appeared to be indifferent to His parents' frantic emotions. When they discovered he was missing, they felt understandable panic and rushed back to Jerusalem, scared to death something had happened to Jesus.

His mildly reproachful response to them when they found Him in the temple seems cold and insensitive: "You should have known that I would be in my Father's house." The words must have resounded in Mary's mind. *What did He mean? Why did He refer to the temple as His Father's house?*

I love the phrase, "His mother stored all these things in her heart." Perhaps this was Jesus's way of beginning to prepare His mother for the time when He would leave her. But at that time,

in that setting, the idea was more than Mary could comprehend for her twelve-year-old boy.

I don't believe we can interpret Jesus as being intentionally disrespectful in the temple. But for just a moment, He revealed His "for this I was born" mission. His calling was to teach the people and ultimately reveal Himself as the long-awaited Messiah. But that fullness of understanding would come sometime later, and in the meantime, Mary would ponder it all in her heart.

The second scriptural passage that might be seen as Jesus abandoning His mother is Luke 8:19–21.

> Once when Jesus' mother and brothers came to see him, they couldn't get to him because of the crowds. Someone told Jesus, "Your mother and your brothers are outside and they want to see you." Jesus replied, "My mother and my brothers are all those who hear the message of God and obey it."

We've jumped ahead in time and find Jesus beginning to live out the purpose for which He came to earth. But again we see that Mary did not recognize "the time is now" moment. She was a loving and concerned mother who couldn't get through the crowds to be with her son.

When He didn't immediately clear the way for her and instead identified everyone there as His family, another huge ponder moment occurred for Mary. Jesus had separated from His mother to do that for which He came. His life and calling

were still a bit of a puzzle to His mother, but even so, she wanted to maintain her connection to Him.

There is something particularly noteworthy about Jesus's timing as we look at His example of how and when He separated from His mother. In the first example, when twelve-year-old Jesus was in the temple, He yielded to His earthly parents and returned to Nazareth with them. However, in the passage we just read, an older Jesus did not yield to His earthly mother but to His heavenly Father and the call He'd been given. The time had come. His spiritual commitment took precedence over His earthly allegiance to His mother and family.

Do you suppose Jesus's response as Mary tried to reach Him through the crowd felt like abandonment to her? It must have been startling to her, yet it surely became another pondering moment as she let go of the leash. I can imagine it may have felt like abandonment, but it really wasn't.

We want to remember that to abandon is to withdraw one's support and responsibility; to desert. Jesus did not desert His mother. Later He showed His support and responsibility for Mary as He hung dying on the cross. In spite of His own agonizing pain, He showed concern for His mother. We read in John 19:26–27, "When Jesus saw his mother standing there beside the disciple he loved, he said to her, 'Woman, he is your son.' And he said to this disciple, 'She is your mother.' And from then on this disciple took her into his home." (The word *woman* in this passage can sound harsh to our ears, but in Aramaic it is a word meant to show respect.)

Jesus's commitment to live out His calling required Him to separate from His mother. In the same way, separating from our mothers is crucial for all of us so we can live out our calling. We each have a calling sovereignly ordained by God. Jesus is a good model for us as we see Him honoring His mother but also separating from her in order to fulfill that for which He came to earth.

LEAVING MOTHER TO LIVE OUT GOD'S CALL

Some of you may be wondering about your personal calling in life. We have great gratitude and respect for Jesus, who had the highest calling in the history of all creation: to be its Savior. "But," you may say, "I hardly have a call of that magnitude. I simply want to get married—that's hardly a call!"

Being married or not being married can indeed be a calling. So can having children or having no children, working outside the home or being a full-time mom, traveling on a job or staying in an office, working out of your home or being president of something, sewing drapes, cooking at the school cafeteria, finding a cure for cancer, or creating a better meat thermometer. Dare I say, your calling in life lies not in *what* you do but in *who* you are?

Remember this. Scripture says God created us for the express purpose of giving Himself the joy of loving us. In being loved, we return that love. That is who we are: persons loved by God. When we return His love, we do it in a spirit of response that

produces service to Him. That is what our relationship with Him is all about. If we do things for God because we are trying to do a payback, we miss the point of the relationship. We are not asked to *earn* the relationship; we are asked to *receive* the relationship.

So then what is the call for each of our lives? To receive God's love and return God's love. We can experience that in everything we do. I realize that sounds far too simple because many of us twirl about trying to figure out where God wants us and what He wants us to do. I do not minimize the importance of that twirl. Many worthy books and articles are written on this subject. (My favorite, incidentally, is the elegant and thought-provoking book entitled *The Call* by Os Guinness.) But at the core of all our searching for our personal call is our response to Jesus, who said, "Follow me."

So then, your call is to love God and serve Him. That service may occur in seemingly nondramatic ways like marriage, children, church activities, and a bowling team. It might also be to go to a foreign country where you literally give your life to helping others and teaching them there is a God who adores them.

You may be asking about now, What does responding to God's call on my life have to do with separating from Mother? I know this feels like a huge stretch for our thinking, but the point is, like Jesus, we cannot allow Mother to keep us from living out our calling.

For example, if you feel called to serve God in a foreign country to work with AIDS victims and your mother is afraid

for your health and begging you not to go, she needs to drop the leash. For you, the time has come. Mother needs to honor your call. She needs to allow you to separate from her call and follow your own.

Suppose you are in a business that has produced a good income and you decide you want to leave the corporate world and take a position in a Christian organization. You will make far less money, but you long to do something with purpose beyond a paycheck. Your mother strongly advises against it because she prefers you to be financially secure. The biggest problem for Mother, however, is that the new job will necessitate a move to another state. Perhaps now is the time.

One of the most common as well as hurtful tensions that occurs with leaving Mother has to do with the marriage of her adult children. If ever there is a mandatory time for Mother to drop the leash, it's when the marital promise is made to "leave and cleave." Marriage is a sacred call. God never designed marriage for three: husband, wife, and mother. It was designed for two: husband and wife.

It is appropriate for mothers to hover over their toddlers as they learn to navigate their ever-expanding world of new sights, sounds, and smells. But mother-hover that continues on into adulthood can be destructive to a marriage. When her children marry, their mother has launched them. They now must continue the journey for themselves. There will undoubtedly be mistakes, but mistakes can be as instructive as a college degree. My word to you mothers who can't seem to drop the leash is get

a job, go back to school, read to the blind, deliver meals on wheels. In other words, find other ways to feel productive and needed. Step back and love your ex-children unconditionally, but from a position of one who knows when to be quiet and when to take a trip. You'll know when the time comes; so will they. Please don't resist that event; recognize it, and let it happen.

Separating from a Mother's Wishes

I have Luci Swindoll's permission to use her relationship with her mother as an illustration of her battle for separation. Luci had to stand firm in her decision to separate from her mother's wishes for her. Luci did not abandon her mother. She abandoned her mother's wishes. The battle revolved around the fact that Luci did not want the same things for her life as her mother wanted for Luci's life.

She says there never was a time when she wanted to settle down in some little Texas town, marry, and have children. Luci wanted to travel all over the world, see everything there was to see, and experience everything there was to experience as long as it wasn't immoral or boring. Her mother did not see any reason for Luci to go to college and certainly didn't think she needed to see the world. Mother's call for Luci was to be a stay-in-town wife and mother. Luci's call was to send postcards from Rome, Vienna, and Paris. Mother had to drop the leash. If she didn't, she wouldn't get postcards.

Our call in life may be to simply and quietly demonstrate

to those in our world that God's love is real and available to those who choose it. Following what may appear to be our human inclinations does not mean our call has been diluted. Those human inclinations are what define us as individuals who happen to be one-of-a-kind creations, like wildflowers that show such a marvelous variety of color, size, and beauty. Luci blooms differently than her mother did.

Luci has left a trail of loving examples about God's existence all over the world. She continues to live out her call to experience the life God gave her and to share that life with others. Fortunately, Luci's mother came to appreciate all that defined her forever-single daughter and ultimately bragged enthusiastically about her accomplishments—which did not include a husband and children. Luci's mother was wise to drop the leash, and Luci was wise to live out her call.

KNOWING BETTER THAN TO PICK UP THE LEASH AGAIN

I experienced a time with Beth when she wanted me to pick up the leash again. I didn't think it would be wise to do so, but I must admit I did struggle with the temptation. But ultimately, I knew it wasn't my call. I'll give you some background.

Beth grew up, married, and had two children; eight years ago, to my utter delight, the family moved to Palm Desert, California, where I was living, and settled in only five minutes away from me. I was able to seriously live out my grandmothering philosophy of

teaching grandsons Alec and Ian all the bad habits I could conjure up. (You know what I mean: dessert before dinner, bubble-gum chewing during church, belching whenever and wherever . . . There's more, but you get the picture. Happily for me, the boys were quick learners.)

I knew Beth was experiencing marital challenges but didn't fully know the extent of its rupture until she took the boys and moved into an apartment. We all had heavy hearts; we talked and cried a lot.

I was also aware of the temptation to do the mother-hover as the relationship between Beth and her husband continued to break further and further apart. I was loving and supportive, but she needed to make her own decision free of my opinions one way or the other. I may have wanted, at times, to pick up the leash, but I could not let myself do it. I cared very much for Beth's husband and understood that their dynamic was complex, but I could not be their therapist. They had to determine their individual path, whether it ultimately rejoined or continued to separate. I could listen, but I dared not direct. That was not my job. It was not my call. Now she thanks me for dropping the leash. But then, she wanted me to tell her what to do.

Because I travel nearly every weekend from April to November during the Women of Faith conference schedule, I felt bad being gone so much. Beth was a counselor in the school district where her dad had been superintendent before his death. She had a wonderful support system and was well known and highly regarded. Nevertheless, I felt I abandoned her every weekend by virtue of my traveling. I wanted her to be cushioned in a more constant environment of love and support. So I bought her and the boys tickets to go to Marion, Ohio, for the summer. Marion was where her biological parents lived. It would be a good distraction for the boys and an emotionally safe place for Beth.

After Beth had been in Marion only a few weeks, I received a jolting phone call from her. Her voice was shaky, and she kept apologizing for what she was about to tell me. In some odd way I could never explain even to myself, I knew what she was struggling to say. But I said nothing of my premonition; I suppose I was hoping I was wrong. Then she said it. In a rush of words she blurted out, "Mom, I accepted a job offer today. The job is here in Marion. I'll work in several public school settings as a counselor and also counsel in a state-supported clinic with ties to the hospital."

"Sweet baby," I whispered, "I don't know why, but for some reason I'm not surprised."

Holding tightly to her emotions, she continued, "And, Mom, . . . I found a house. It's perfect for the boys and me. You'll love it, Mom. It has huge elm trees in the backyard, and there's a perfect tree for you to sit under and read."

For a moment we both cried softly. Then I told her, "If you've got the tree, baby, I've got the book."

The decision to move was an agonizing one for Beth. She was wracked with feelings of guilt about leaving me several states behind. She had guilt about moving into the community where her biological family lived and beginning what could look like an abandonment of her old family in deference for the new one. She feared she was showing some kind of disrespect for "all I'd done for her" and that her move was selfish and insensitive.

My heart ached for Beth as all her troubled emotions came spilling out. She did not deserve the guilt feelings, not one of them. My call had been to be her mother in whatever time frame God had ordained. My call was also to respect the amazing unfolding of what He was doing in both our lives. This was no wild plan that slipped through the netting of God's sovereign design. From the beginning of time, it was meant to occur.

On the other hand, if you think for one minute I congratulated God on His creativity as I watched Beth move from California to Ohio, you give me more credit than I deserve. I didn't say I *liked* the plan; I said I recognized God's sovereign design. The reality is, I didn't like it then, and I don't like it now. But I have grace for it. Why?

I believe with all my heart that God not only directs my steps, He is also deeply invested in developing my character. Perhaps there's no better training ground for that than mothering. As a mother, I have no right to interfere with the God-mandated "leave-and-cleave" principle. I must let my children leave, and it is their choice to whom or what they cleave. I don't always like that principle, but I know it's right. God does not make any mistakes. And when we make them, He has promised to make good come from them.

When It's Time for
Ex-Children to Come Back

We opened this chapter with the question, "When is an acceptable time for ex-kids to leave their mother?" I hope this discussion has shed some light on that question. But now in closing, let me ask another question: "When is the acceptable time to come back to Mother?"

My suggested answer is when Mother is no longer responsible for herself. The key is knowing the difference between "to" and "for." We are responsible "to" show Mother love, respect, kindness, and compassion. But when you need to take responsibility "for" her, it means she is no longer able to do that for herself. My ex-children will know that time has come when I start humming loudly during communion, drop a trail of food wrappers throughout the grocery store, and then leave before paying because I'm no longer hungry. Or if I begin a mindless stare at my meat thermometer, they'll know. They'll know the time is now.

✺

nine

WHEN IT FEELS
LIKE GOD IS GONE

The LORD will work out his plans for my life—
for your faithful love, O LORD, endures forever.
Don't abandon me, for you made me.
—PSALM 138:8

Some years ago my grandson Ian and I were having a rock-kicking contest as we made the five-minute walk from his house to downtown Carmel, California. He's always been a deep thinker, so the question he asked me that day as a four-year-old seemed typical of him.

"Maungya, do you ever wonder where God is?" I could have answered any number of ways: He's in my heart. He's also in nature. In fact He shows up everywhere and in everything. But instead, I flipped the question back to him: "Where do you think He is, Ian?"

There was a brief silence as he evaluated whether or not my rock had fallen short of his. Then in a conspiratorial voice he told me, "God is gone. I haven't told Mama or even Adam, but I have it on good 'assortity' he's gone." (Adam was Ian's friend, and *assortity* was his word for *authority*. I don't know where he learned the phrase, but he used it all the time. His mispronunciation of the word never failed to charm me.)

When I probed him about the idea as well as his "assortity," Ian's response was simply, "He's just gone, Maungya, and that's all there is to say." As we made our way to Carmel's main street, we ran out of rocks to kick, but if there had been any, Ian reminded me, I shouldn't kick them because I might hurt someone.

I couldn't quite let our "God is gone" conversation drop so abruptly. I told Ian I had it on good authority that God was living in my heart. He patted my hand condescendingly as we entered the ice cream store, saying only, "Do you want your usual chocolate, Maungya?"

TRACING THE ROOT OF LIFE'S POTENTIAL FOR ABANDONMENT

What captured my attention on that rock-kicking walk was the sense Ian had of life's potential for abandonment. This is the same little man who informed his friend Adam that I had "got left" as an explanation for my solo visits to Ian's house. These heavy-duty ponderings were going on in a kid who was only four years old. Where did they come from? His parents were still together, and Beth did not work outside the home. So why was he so aware of abandonment potential? Why did it even occur to him if he had not really experienced it?

I believe Ian's four-year-old expression of potential abandonment had its root in what we all have experienced: we have all left the perfect womb, with all its effortless and need-meeting perfection. This womb-abandonment is traumatizing and leaves an imprint that is never eliminated from our great memory storehouse. We don't consciously remember it, but our thinking and sometimes our behavior reflect its continual presence.

Perhaps to some of us such negative, womb-abandonment thoughts and feelings seem to exist as a cloud of pessimism or a dark hole of depression. Perhaps only a four-year-old dares to express that primal memory that can feel so serious, it makes us think that even God leaves.

But this primal memory of abandonment has a tracer we can follow back even further. Let's remember what we read about the Garden of Eden. It had womb-like perfection. There was no tension or worry about needs; all needs were met. Food, water, beauty, companionship, and total peace were all provided, requiring absolutely no effort from Adam and Eve. They could lie around all day, feeding each other grapes. To say they had it made is an understatement. To say they existed in paradise is biblical. What were they thinking when they disobeyed God?

Because of what they were thinking and because of what they did, all humanity was forever disconnected from that original womb paradise. The Eden umbilical cord was cut. God's sobering words to Adam were, "All your life you will sweat to produce food, until your dying day. Then you will return to the ground from which you came. For you were made from dust, and to the dust you will return" (Genesis 3:19).

Scripture says God cursed the ground and banished Adam and Eve from paradise. The question is, Did that banishment bring with it abandonment from God?

To be *banished* is to be removed . . . not left. While Adam and Eve's banishment from Eden certainly brought abandonment of effortless living, did God actually leave His first created ones to live a cursed and abandoned existence? Do we experience His abandonment when we sin and later wonder, *What was I thinking?*

In spite of the imprint we all carry (that imprint being the inclination to sin), God does not curse us and leave. I have it on good authority.

Why God Asks, "Where Are You?"

Let's do a quick replay of the post-apple scene in the garden. Because Adam and Eve had eaten of the tree of the knowledge of good and evil, they knew they had done a "bad thing." Genesis 3:8–9 describes their shame: "Toward evening they heard the LORD God walking about in the garden, so they hid themselves among the trees. The LORD God called to Adam, 'Where are you?'"

The point here is not their hiding in shame; we all do that

when we've done a bad thing. The point here is that God came looking for them; He sought them out with the question, "Where are you?" God didn't ask the question because He didn't know where they were. He asked the question so that they might *admit* where they were. He also asked the question so they could choose to respond to Him—or try to avoid Him by remaining hidden. They chose to come out of hiding.

When they did so, God did the most amazingly nurturing thing: "And the LORD God made clothing from animal skins for Adam and his wife" (3:21). They had not known shame before they disobeyed, but having done so, they needed clothes.

So here's what we have on good authority: God seeks us out, even when we've made bad choices. He does not leave us to sink deeper and deeper into our chosen messes. Instead, He comes after us, asking for our response to the question, "Where are you?" He does not ever sever the inseparable bonds He wraps around us.

In my heart, I accept that "good authority." I believe God never leaves us. Yet there was a time when I briefly sided with Ian and his "good assortity" concerning the supposition that God is gone. That supposition became personal to my life as I saw my mother grapple with the loss of His presence. The familiar cry, "Where is God?" gave way to the disillusioned whisper, "He is gone."

My mom was my priest. She taught me Scripture. She taught me moral and ethical principles, and she introduced me to Jesus when I was five years old. I always knew she was not

God, but she seemed like it much of the time. I confused her with God because she was patient, long-suffering, and gentle. She never raised her voice; I always felt her love.

Though she was far more seriously inclined than I, she loved to laugh, and there were many times we literally fell into a heap laughing together. During a tour of John Knox's house in Edinburgh, Scotland, we both got giggly over the guide who droned his way through all the rooms of the house explaining its distinctive architectural features with zero personality. The only animation he exhibited was an unmistakable ocular tic that would occasionally punctuate the ends of his sentences. I was finding his tic a distraction, but because I was hard up for entertainment, I fought valiantly against an inappropriate desire to giggle. Apparently my mother was struggling with the same impulse. When I heard the muffled little snort stuffed deeply in her throat, I couldn't control myself. I let out my unattractive hoot-laugh, and it was all over for both of us. We were formally asked to leave. We leaned against the side of John Knox's house and together experienced the healing power of laughter. (Inappropriate laughter provides more healing than the socially acceptable kind. I have it on good assortity.)

My mother was raised in a highly educated environment where "doing good things" was stressed and contributing to the betterment of society was a personal commitment. The Bible was considered to be no more than a collection of aphorisms and occasional bits of good poetry. During the completion of Mom's graduate work in Berkeley, she came to know not only that God loved her but that He sent His Son Jesus to provide salvation for her. Her decision to receive Jesus into her heart and mind became the defining moment of her entire life. Mom was an intellectual, so to receive Jesus into her heart as well as her mind was a monumental change for her thinking.

She went to Nyack College and Seminary in New York so that she might learn more about the Bible. In so doing, she met my father. He felt called to the ministry, and together they forged out a philosophy of their life's work. My mother believed whether one has a PhD or a grade-school diploma, human need is the same. It's the same in sophisticated cities; it's the same in rural communities. All people are broken in one way or another, and all people need to be directed to the Great Physician. They married and spent a lifetime sharing that ministry.

My mother taught me about prayer. I learned from her words, but I learned even more by her example. There was something about Mom's quiet dignity that somehow coupled with God's majesty. I know that sounds a bit lofty, but I don't know how else to describe what I observed as well as experienced. When Mom retreated into "her room" and prayed, somehow change came about. Dad, the pastor, was out there making it happen, but Mom was "in there" praying it to happen. Their different approaches for achieving the same goal fascinated me. They seemed to work in harmony.

When I was a sophomore at Seattle Pacific University, my roommate, Karen Petersen, reminded me of my mother. Karen was extremely bright, gentle, loving, patient, and had a fascinating prayer life. Karen and I, like Mom and I, had frequent deep conversations, many of which were about prayer. I was stunned to learn that Karen believed in speaking in tongues. Her mother was an Assembly of God pastor, and a more compelling and tender witness for Jesus I have never met, except of course, my own mother. Karen and her mother gave tremendous credibility to a practice I thought was weird and my father had warned me against when I left for college.

During Christmas break from Seattle Pacific I had my first opportunity to run those speaking-in-tongues thoughts past my mother. I told her how much I admired Karen, how spiritually in touch she seemed, and how responsive I was to Karen's mother. Finally I asked Mom, "What do you think of the whole *tongues* thing?"

Quietly, as always, she said, "Well, Marilyn, it's been my practice for over thirty years."

I looked at her in total disbelief. Falteringly I asked, "Does Daddy know?" Her response—"He doesn't seem to"—sent me into an hour-long wall stare.

So that explained it. I didn't fully understand it then and I don't fully understand it now, but there was a dose of spiritual high octane in my mother that I relied on and thanked God for; so did my father. I had always been a bit in awe of my mother's intellect, but then I was even more in awe over her spiritual experience and how it evidenced itself in her life.

With this bit of history, you can understand then how incomprehensible it was for me several years later to come into the shocking witness of my mother's "dark night of the soul." She was seventy-two when the headaches began. They were accompanied by excruciating pain in her left arm. The other pain jumped around, but the headaches stayed put. The normal activities of life—eating, sleeping, walking, thinking—had all become functions that were sometimes beyond her ability.

The doctors couldn't agree on a diagnosis. Had there been a stroke that left nerve damage? Was there a brain tumor causing diminished brain function? Was she just showing signs of aging with symptoms that resisted medication? There were several surgeries, but nothing seemed to help.

I could hardly bear the look of physical anguish I saw in my mother's face. There were several prayer chains that faithfully brought her debilitating pain to the attention of the Great Physician. Many prayed for direct healing; others prayed for her endurance. I prayed that God be fair. I expected Him to be.

After four years of watching my mother suffer the debilitating headaches and body pain, I began to lose faith in God's system of justice. What Mom was experiencing was not fair; she deserved so much more after her years of loving service to God. He could reverse those pain channels and give her body peace. She could die, but why should she die in such physical devastation? She had been such a saint, not just to me, but to countless others as well.

One morning my father called and said Mom had been rushed to the hospital the night before. She had walked out of her bathroom and handed him an empty bottle. Earlier it had been full of sleeping pills. "I've just swallowed them all," she said.

After having her stomach pumped, she was in a weakened condition but the doctor said she would recover.

As I frantically drove the two hours from my house to be with her in San Diego, I was aware of a huge shift of new emotions veering over to the edge of my soul. I needed now to be strong, but instead I felt desperate and helpless. Mother had always been my rock. She had always been my mentor, confidant, intercessor, the cushion I slumped into when I felt weak.

I tried yet again to think through how agonizing her life had become. I had watched pain cloud her vision and confuse her thoughts. Her mind, which had been her greatest human asset, had now led her down an unrecognizable path. She had attempted the unthinkable.

I sat next to Mom's hospital bed constantly stroking her hand, her cheek, her hair. She acknowledged me by squeezing my hand occasionally, but otherwise she was silent. Hours later, when I got ready to leave, she opened her eyes, looked at me, and said, "I'm so sorry. I have failed you, your father, and God. Please forgive me."

In a rush of words I assured her she need not ask my forgiveness, that I loved her and would always love her. Her only response was to say, "I don't want anyone to know about this. I'm so embarrassed." At her request, we never spoke of it again. This is the first time I have told her story.

So why am I telling it now? Perhaps knowing Mother's story will help you realize there are times when God asks the question,

"Where are you?" and, out of shame, you don't respond. You remain hidden; you're embarrassed by something you did.

God wants us to feel safe enough to answer, to tell Him what He already knows. Why? He wants to maintain our connection. He wants us to feel the inseparable bond that melds Him to us. He wants to assure us that He "will work out his plans for our lives."

For my mother, pain was the big disconnector; it seemed to disconnect her from God. She had lost mental clarity as well as spiritual clarity. God knew that and did not judge her; neither did He leave her. I don't think she knew that, though, until He took her to be with Him two months later. She died of pneumonia. Now she knows what she didn't know then.

ABANDONING OUR EXPECTATIONS OF GOD

If we have it on good authority that God does not abandon us, why does it so frequently feel that He does? Is that feeling of abandonment simply because we lost two great wombs and we just can't seem to get over it? Or because we go through difficult times and seem to lose our way?

Certainly the loss of two security-producing wombs has imprinted the psyches of us all, but so too does the fear of hearing the silence of God. Wracked with pain or devastated by grief or crushed by failure, we think that when God appears to be indifferent to our needs and prayers, He must have gone away. He must have left us.

What is that about?

We have expectations of God. For one thing, most of us think it makes sense to be rewarded for good behavior. We expect God thinks that too. When we're good, doing all the "right things," we expect God to notice and protect us as well as reward us. When He does not always do that, we may be tempted to grumble, but we won't grumble loudly or noticeably because that would not be the right thing to do. We wait, though. We wait for our reward.

My friend Ney Bailey has a darling little dog named Bailey. (Not until this moment did I realize Bailey shares his mama's last name. I've got to ask her about that.) At any rate, Bailey knows how to work the reward system. Every time he does the "right thing," he gets a treat. He's caught on that always being "good dog" will bring reward; he rarely is not a good dog.

Last week I promised Ney I would drop by her house while she was at the dentist and let Bailey out to do his "business." It was an easy favor to grant. What I forgot was Bailey is used to being rewarded for the successful completion of his business. As I was getting ready to leave for home, Bailey followed me to the door with an unmistakable look of reproach on his little furry face. I thought, *He wants some cuddle time. I don't need to be in such a hurry.* So I dropped to the floor. I stroked him, flattered him, and talked baby-talk to him. All to no avail. He backed off from me and continued to look at me as if I had committed an unpardonable sin.

Then it dawned on me. He had done his business, and I had

not rewarded him. I had indeed committed the unpardonable sin! His attitude toward me changed completely when he got his reward. He was good, and I was good. What a good neighborhood!

I know this sounds so elementary, and maybe I'm only talking to myself, but this kind of reward system is what I have often expected from God. And that's just not how God works.

I have a friend who has served as a doctor in several clinics in North Africa. She is sixty-five and has never married; she cheerfully states she's married to God and medicine. Her spirit is always upbeat and fun. And she has just tested positive for the HIV/AIDS virus.

I can't help asking, "Why, God? She is so good and has served You with such dedication and devotion. Where is her reward? She deserves better. Why couldn't she come back to the U.S. and live out her remaining years in retirement puttering in a garden and training a puppy to be a good dog? Why couldn't we have tea in my kitchen like we used to before she went to Africa?"

One of the mind-sets I've needed to abandon throughout my life has been my expectations of God. I know all that great scripture about God's ways not being my ways, but it's hard for me to swallow the fact that He does not always seem fair. (I know. I'll never get a reward for talk like that.)

Now I too know what I didn't know then. By abandoning my expectation of God and realizing I can't coerce His mystery into a predictable formula based upon the merit system, I free up more space in my mind for His ways. And because His ways are not my ways, I have to choose to let Him be God and rest in His invitation to trust Him. I don't always do that well, but I know it is the only path to peace. It is the ultimate solution for our fears of abandonment.

We can't any of us go to Eden or to that cushy place that housed us for nine months, but we can all go to the womb of heaven. It is there we experience unending peace, connection, satisfaction, and freedom from all want. Once there, we will know beyond a shadow of a doubt that God is not gone. We have that on good authority.

> I have called you by name; you are mine. When you go through deep waters and great trouble, I will be with you. When you go through rivers of difficulty, you will not drown! (Isaiah 43:1–2)

ten

☀

LEFT WAITING BY
UNANSWERED PRAYER

*And we can be confident that he will listen to us
whenever we ask him for anything in line with his will.
And if we know he is listening when we make our requests,
we can be sure that he will give us what we ask for.*

—1 JOHN 5:14—15

As a child I desperately wanted brown eyes. It seemed rea-
sonable to me to make that a subject of prayer. But after
much spiritual diligence, I came to the conclusion God was
not going to do a color switch for me. The result of that unanswered prayer was a minor crisis of faith. Did He or did He not
answer prayer? I came to the unsettling conclusion that maybe
He did not.

The conclusion was unsettling because the promise was
right there in the Bible. Look at 1 John 5:14–15 again in the
epigraph above. It sounds pretty clear, doesn't it? We are assured

God is listening to us when we pray and that He will give us what we ask for. And that's just one of several scriptures that tell us the same thing. For example, Matthew 7:7 says, "Keep on asking, and you will be given what you ask for."

Or consider James 4:2: "The reason you don't have what you want is that you don't ask God for it." When we ask, God answers.

Somerset Maugham, the eighteenth-century English novelist, wrote poignantly in his novel *Of Human Bondage* about a boy named Philip who had just read a similar scripture in Mark's Gospel, which says, "You can pray for anything, and if you believe, you will have it" (11:24).

Philip was inspired to believe that God would heal his clubfoot. Listen in on his interior monologue:

> He would be able to play football. His heart leaped as he saw himself running faster than any of the other boys. At the end of Easter term there were the sports, and he would be able to go in for the races; he rather fancied himself over the hurdles. It would be splendid to be like everyone else, not to be stared at curiously by new boys who did not know about his deformity, nor at the baths in summer to need incredible precautions, while he was undressing, before he could hide his foot in the water.
>
> He prayed with all the power in his soul. No doubts assailed him. He was confident in the Word of God. And the night before he was to go back to school he went up to bed tremulous with excitement. There

was snow on the ground and Aunt Louise had allowed herself the unaccustomed luxury of a fire in her bedroom, but in Philip's little room it was so cold that his fingers were numb, and he had great difficulty undoing his collar. His teeth chattered. The idea came to him that he must do something more unusual to attract the attention of God, and he turned back the rug which was in front of his bed so that he could kneel on the bare boards, and then it struck him that his nightshirt was a softness that might displease his Maker, so he took it off and said his prayers naked.

When he got into bed he was so cold that for some time he could not sleep, but when he did, it was so soundly that Mary Ann had to shake him when she brought his hot water in the morning. She talked to him while she drew the curtains, but he did not answer; he had remembered at once that this was the morning of the miracle. His heart was filled with joy and gratitude. His first instinct was to put down his hand and feel the foot which was whole now. But to do this seemed to doubt the goodness of God. He knew that his foot was well.

But at last he made up his mind, and with the toes of his right foot he just touched his left. Then he passed his hand over it. He limped downstairs just as Mary Ann was going into the dining room for prayers, and then he sat down to breakfast. "You're very quiet this morning, Philip," said Aunt Louisa presently.

This story excerpt rips my heart because we have all experienced a sometimes mind-numbing, soul-thudding jolt of disillusionment when God does not give us what we ask for, and as a result we may choose to abandon the faith because it appears God abandoned our prayer. It seems to mean that either He does not truly hear or He does not truly care. For those of us who don't choose either of those responses, it means there's more we need to know about God, and more we need to know about prayer.

What We Need to Know about God

Let's first talk about what we need to know about God. My heart breaks over the fictional character of Philip simply because I've been there. I haven't stripped down to naked misery on a freezing cold floor in my supplication to God, but I have tried to make myself worthy of His ear in other ways. I have frequently felt I had to earn the right to be heard and in so doing present to Him my well-practiced spiritual face.

What is that face? One of the spiritual faces is to quote scripture to God while I'm presenting my prayer case. That does not seem questionable . . . until I realize I'm expecting God to be more inclined to hear me as He notices I'm quoting by memory. I've taken the time to memorize God's Word and repeat it back to Him, and in so doing I surely earn myself some bargaining chips. There is very little difference between that kind of prayer and Philip's tooth-chattering prayer exhibiting relentless belief that his clubfoot would be healed.

Another face I've presented, which is much like Philip's, is to refuse to indicate to God that I lack faith that my request will be granted. This face has me believing if I falter in my humanity, I would be faltering in front of God. He then would see that I am one of those "Oh-ye-of-little-faith" persons and perhaps would choose not to grant my request. So I refuse to even consider that my prayer will not be answered. I dare not imply to myself or anyone else an alternative view. To do so would warn God that I am faithless.

The problem with presenting to God a seemingly unflinching position of faith is that it constantly puts me on the performance treadmill. Thinking I can present to God one face while at times feeling another is tiring. It is also ridiculous. Prayer is not about performance. It's about talking to God. Every now and then I have to re-know what I know: God is my Father; I am His child. I approach Him as I am, and sometimes as I am is childish. Nowhere does Scripture say I can only talk to Him when I'm altogether and show signs of great maturity. The requirement God has for my coming to Him in prayer is . . . that I come to Him in prayer. That's all there is to it. When my faith falters, I need to tell Him what He already knows instead of childishly hoping He won't notice my faith defect or my jumping through hoops trying to impress Him.

But after coming to Him in honest and nonmanipulative ways, what happens to our faith when we receive what appears to be an unreasonable divine prayer refusal? How do we then relate to God? Do you suppose Philip's faith in an all-giving, need-providing God dissolved in despair and disbelief at the discovery that his foot remained as it was before he prayed?

Unless I've backslidden into my spiritual face thing, I will relate to God in a way that generally reflects how I am honestly feeling about Him. When His divine refusal breaks my heart, I can feel insecure about His love for me. I don't stop believing He exists; there is too much evidence that points to His existence for me to question whether or not there is a God. But His prayer silence or prayer refusal is at times a challenge to my conviction about my being the object of His unfailing love.

I have been a believer for more than sixty years. That means I've prayed about a gazillion issues, starting with my childish request for brown eyes. Many of my most deeply felt and fervent prayer requests have been denied. I prayed for the healing of our baby Joanie, born with spina bifida, for my parents, and for my husband, but they all died. So where does that leave me? Have I spent all those years feeling uncertain and insecure? From time to time I have, but I think I'm finally coming to terms with what appears to me to be unanswered prayer and the feelings of abandonment that accompany it. Have I stopped praying? No. But I've changed how I pray and how I think about prayer.

Changing How I Feel about Prayer

Let me share a personal experience that I hope will illustrate this change. I am, as of this writing, experiencing an annoying yet painful health issue; I have shingles. This is a most peculiar malady; why it is called shingles is beyond me. My skin looks more like Spanish tiles that shingles, but maybe I just have a more Continental variety. Two weeks ago during brunch on Sunday I asked my group the question, "Does anyone here know anything about shingles? I think maybe I'm getting them."

There was an immediate look of concern as each person assured me shingles were awful and that I did not want them. Whether I wanted them or not ceased to be a choice when several days later my doctor assured me I had them.

Whenever my loved ones have been "standing in the need of prayer," as the old hymn says, I've been fervent in my prayer language. I've longed to be heard and to see God do beyond what I could ask or think (see Isaiah 55:8 and Ephesians 3:20). Were these heart cries to God inappropriate, excessive, selfish, or immature? No. I was simply being human, and in being human I presented my heart to my heavenly Father.

But I'm not presenting my heart to my heavenly Father regarding my shingles. I'm not praying about this malady that is not only excessively uncomfortable externally but also affects my internal being in odd ways. I feel the hint of flu that does no more than hint. There is a slight feel of being chilled that does not require a sweater but causes me to close my patio door. My skin hurts even in places where my spanish tiles are not showing. The hurt is not enough to make me avoid human touch, but I'm aware now of how frequently people do a backslap as they hug.

So why am I not praying about my shingles when I did pray

for my loved ones? Desperation, I guess. I pray fervently when I'm desperate. When I'm desperate I have to fully submit to God's control and not mine. I have no control when I'm desperate. I was helpless in the face of my loved ones' need, so I cried out to God. I'm not crying out to God about my shingles because I don't feel helpless. I seem to be thinking I can "push through them" because they haven't knocked me flat. I pray fervently when I'm knocked flat.

I don't like that about me.

I think there's another reason I'm not praying about my shingles. I don't want to make a big deal of them because I don't want to feel the disappointment that may come if God doesn't do anything about them. Those insecurities about God are left-over feelings from what felt like prayer abandonment years ago. Unfortunately, those feelings lurk about in my soul and cause me to try and avoid disappointment.

As I confess my faltering humanity to you, I know better than to base my faith on feelings. The problem with feelings is they have no brains. When I take my brainless approach to prayer, which is to not pray about some issues to ward off potential disappointment, I need to activate my brain and pray from what I *know* and not what I *feel*. I know Scripture teaches that God welcomes my cry, hears my cry, and promises to never leave me as I cry. That's a flat-out promise. Nevertheless, some of our experiences produce "yeah buts" that continue to mutter in our brains. Our "yeah buts" make more sense to us than God's promise to stay with us.

For example, Somerset Maugham was basing his lack of faith on a boyhood experience of prayer rejection. Like the character Philip in *Of Human Bondage,* Maugham prayed that his stuttering would be healed. The character of Philip illustrated the disillusionment of the book's author.

Saint Augustine was also disillusioned as he prayed that his teachers at school would stop beating him for various minor infractions of the rules. His prayers did not ward off the severe school punishments he received. Instead, the abuse continued.

A perfect example of one who prayed in spite of what he felt and experienced was Job. In spite of his experience, he refused to abandon his faith. It was his friends who provided the yeah buts as they tried to figure out why Job's calamities had buried him in losses and why God had not responded to his prayer for deliverance. They came up with a bunch of speculations for why Job was in the mess he was in and why God seemed to have targeted him.

God, in His one-on-0ne talk with Job, dismissed every one of those speculations as nonsense and not worth the air the words floated on.

So what was the answer God gave to Job about the source of his afflictions and the reason for God's abandonment no? God didn't give an answer. Instead He challenged Job to look around him and witness God's touch, His power, and His creativity throughout the earth and the universe.

Before Job's God encounter, Job expressed his agony with these words:

Yet when I hoped for good, evil came; when I looked for light, then came darkness. The churning inside me never stops. (Job 30:26–27 NIV)

Job received no answer and no explanations for the relentless churning within himself and the external losses he had experienced. But Job's faith in God remained constant. Yet again, still sitting in sackcloth and ashes with running sores all over his body, he said, "Though he slay me, yet will I trust in him" (Job 13:15 KJV).

You will remember God ultimately restored Job's health as well as the loss of his family and his property. In fact, God gave Job twice as much as he had before calamity struck him down and stripped him bare. Job's restorations may be comforting, but they still don't explain the *why* of what appears at first to be God's indifference to Job's prayers. It does, however, inspire me to trust God, contrary to what I feel or experience.

Changing How I Think about Prayer

Not only am I working to change how I feel about prayer but also what I think about prayer. There are certain realities about life that I have to take into account. To begin with, we all must remember we live in a world totally awash in evil. The source of that evil springs from the enemy who wishes upon us heartache, ruin, and loss of faith in the source of all that is pure. The battle Satan wages against God's people and all He represents is sobering. We are at war. We have been at war since that fateful day in the garden. We cannot blame God for the sin-fallout that engulfs us on this earth. As long as we live here we are candidates for calamity. Also, as long as we live here we are candidates for God's restoration.

Let's take a minute and remind ourselves of what we may already know as we consider the fact that we live on a battleground and not a playground. According to Scripture, Satan has been given certain rights to this earth for a period of time. Though Jesus referred to him as the "prince of this world," Jesus also said that ruler would one day be "cast out" (John 12:31). Satan has limited time here as the world's ruler. While he can, he seeks to destroy our souls and our faith to believe God cares and hears our prayers.

In no uncertain language, Ephesians 6:12 explains what we're up against as we seek to maintain our faith:

> For we do not wrestle against flesh and blood, but against principalities, against powers, against the rulers of the darkness of this age, against spiritual hosts of wickedness in the heavenly places. (NKJV)

Are we then helpless pawns as we live in a world dominated by rulers of darkness and a host of wickedness? Does that environment mean our prayers have little combative power? Not at all. That wickedness is used by a sovereign God for our spiritual good. We need to review 1 Peter 1:7 to understand how God brings our good from Satan's bad:

These trials are only to test your faith, to show that it is strong and pure. It is being tested as fire tests and purifies gold—and your faith is far more precious to God than mere gold. So if your faith remains strong after being tried by fiery trials, it will bring you much praise and glory and honor on the day when Jesus Christ is revealed to the whole world.

The Ultimate Challenge for Our Faith

So this is what I know: you and I experience injustice, pain, hurt, and other calamities that Satan means for our spiritual destruction. God has granted him certain powers over us, so we can say God gives permission for calamity, but He wills us spiritual life from that calamity. Satan wills us spiritual death from that calamity.

Just as the unsettling wager between God and Satan occurred that God might prove Job's unwavering faith would remain intact in spite of calamity, we too are placed in a position to show that our faith will remain intact in spite of our calamity. It all boils down to a matter of faith. Will we trust God even when we don't see the changes we're praying for or when we sense no assurances that God will intervene in the circumstances of our lives? Will our faith hang in there even though it hangs by a thin thread? That is the ultimate challenge for our faith as well as the ultimate determiner of how we pray, in spite of the abandonment.

So then we come back to my shingles. If I avoid praying about them in order to spare myself disappointment, I'm not experiencing faith in God's loving nature, receptive spirit, or sovereign right to do what He has ordained for me. And what *has* He ordained for me? He has ordained that I mature and develop in my trust of who He is and how He is. He has ordained that this current fiery trial produce in me soul-gold and not soul-avoidance.

I believe the line from 1 John 5:14 that says "ask him for anything in line with his will" can be understood not as an effort to examine all our potentially selfish motives and bring them into line with God's will but as a way of knowing God's will is accomplished no matter how human I am in my desires. God wants what is best for me. That is His will. I too want what is best for me, and if what is best for me will be accomplished in spite of what I ask, then I can rest easy, even in the fiery trial, because *God is in the trial.* I can also rest in what has appeared to be unanswered prayer. Prayer is always answered simply because that is what God does. What He does *not* always do is answer my way or according to my timeline.

The Canopy of God's Mystery

As I continually challenge myself to trust God in spite of my prayers not always producing what I want and to remember I am on a battleground where the forces of evil seek to destroy me, I am encouraged on another level of realization. And that is to be content to live under the canopy of God's mystery. There is much I don't know and never will know. There is much I'm not meant to know. Deuteronomy 29:29 says, "There are secrets the LORD your God has not revealed to us" (TLB).

I've never liked secrets unless I'm in on them. God has not let me in on some things He knows, plans, and, in love, means to accomplish for my good. There is an odd sort of comfort to that in spite of my wanting to know His secrets that pertain to me. I'm invited to rest in His mystery and in His love. Ecclesiastes 11:5 further invites me to rest in His mystery as I'm told, "You'll never understand the mystery at work in all that God does" (MSG).

So then, how am I to live in harmony and peace with a God who holds secrets and whose mystery I'll never fully understand? How do I approach this mysterious God with my prayers about the everyday stuff like shingles? I realize I must pray with the same fervency I did for the healing and life extension of my loved ones. I don't yield to the temptation to protect myself in the event my shingles don't go away. I allow myself the luxury of coming to Him and talking to Him about all aspects of this malady, which is now even more challenging than when I started writing this chapter. I also don't wait until I'm desperate to talk to Him. My shingles are a *now* event, and I need to talk to Him in the now.

In coming to God in prayer and laying before Him all my needs as well as desires, my method for doing so is encapsulated in Proverbs 3:5. "Trust in the LORD with all your heart, and lean not on your own understanding" (NKJV). I'm not meant to understand it all. If I did, trust would not be necessary. Understanding would be all I need, but trust is what God needs.

Trust comes to me when I remember what God says about His love for me. Trust also comes as I recognize that His love provides a promise about my circumstances that don't always change when I want them to. About those circumstances, Romans 8:28 says, "And we know that God causes everything to work together for the good of those who love God and are called according to his purpose for them." His purpose for me is that I love and trust Him in all things. His purpose for me is that I stay in constant touch with Him through prayer, whether it's about death or shingles. His invitation is always, "Come unto me, . . . and I will give you rest" (Matthew 11:28 KJV).

I'm doing that right now, and in the doing there is rest.

Part 2

☼

Holding On to What's Left

eleven

✵

DON'T ABANDON
YOUR DREAMS

The seed cast on good earth is the person who . . .
takes in the News, and then produces
a harvest beyond his wildest dreams.
—MATTHEW 13:22–24 (MSG)

Until now, we've talked about abandonment as something
that happens to us—as an action by someone else, intentionally or unintentionally, that strongly impacts our lives. In
many instances, we may not even realize that "getting left" is
the source of some of the emotions and behaviors that affect us
as adults, until we follow the inevitable tracers back to their
root. In most cases, we see that we had no control over what
originally happened. There was, most likely, nothing we could
have done that would have changed what happened. But by
understanding the origin of our feelings, we can change how

we respond *now* to our emotions and behaviors that spring from that event.

Before we end our time together, I want to warn you about two other abandonments that you *can* do something about. In fact, you can prevent these abandonments from happening, because in both cases, *you* are the one who decides whether to "leave." I'm talking about your dreams for your life and your reason for living. I hope you will cherish these two God-given gifts and never abandon them, even when "staying" with them may seem pointless and futile.

First let's talk about holding on to our dreams, and in the next chapter we'll discuss the importance of recognizing and clinging to our reason for living.

The word *dream* can be defined as a "wild fancy or hope." It can also be defined as a "reverie, a trance, or a state of abstraction." The Webster definition I am using is that a dream is "a deep aspiration." I'm also using the word in relation to God's plans for our lives; He has deep aspirations for us, which I often refer to as His dreams for us. With these word specifics in mind, let me tell you about the dream an old southern country preacher had for his teenage son.

Dad thought it was getting time the boy should give some consideration to what profession he might enter. Like many young men, the boy didn't really know what he wanted to do, and he didn't seem too concerned about it. Dad had a dream his son would become a preacher.

One day, while the boy was away at school, his father

decided to try an experiment. He went into his son's room and placed on his study table four objects:

a Bible

a silver dollar

a bottle of whiskey

a *Playboy* magazine

"I'll just hide behind the door," the old preacher said to himself, "when the boy comes home from school this afternoon, I'll see which object he picks up. If it's the Bible, he's going to be a preacher like me, and what a blessing that would be! If he picks up the dollar, he's going to be a businessman, and that would be okay too. But if he picks up the bottle, he's going to be a no-good drunk, and Lord, what a shame that would be. And worst of all, if he picks up that magazine, he's gonna be a skirt-chasin' bum!"

The old man waited anxiously and soon heard his son enter the house, whistling and heading for his room. The boy tossed his books on the bed. Then, as he turned to leave the room, he spotted the objects on the table. With curiosity in his eyes, he walked over to inspect them.

A moment passed, then he picked up the Bible and placed it under his arm. He picked up the silver dollar and dropped it into his pocket. Then he uncorked the bottle and took a long drink while he admired this month's centerfold.

"Lord have mercy," the old preacher disgustedly whispered. "He's gonna be a politician."

It is a common parental preoccupation to have dreams for

our children. Those dreams can come in the form of the old preacher's dream to have his son carry on the family preaching tradition for yet another generation. It can also be communicated to the child that her responsibility is to achieve the dream the parent was not able to achieve. More often than not, the pressure for the child to become what the parent could not be is a subtle pressure, perhaps one not even articulated by the parent and only sensed by the child.

I have only recently realized I have carried my father's personal dream for himself and lived it out for him. I've always thought I was living out my own dream. And actually I *am* living out my own dream, but there has always been in me an inner and often ill-defined sense of urgency to do what I do.

What was Dad's dream for me? That I be highly educated. He came from a "litter of ten" children (his phrase) who grew up in an impoverished background both financially and educationally. Eastern Canada had severe winters; the snow piled high against the buildings. There were not enough shoes in the family to go around, so only one or two could brave the weather and trudge off to school. Because Dad was one of the younger children, his turn for shoes came infrequently. When he was able to attend, he was mesmerized by the letters of the alphabet and how they fit together in various formations to construct words that then created sentences. He loved rhythmic sounds of poetry and the feelings he had as he responded to its beauty. Nevertheless, his hunger to learn was thwarted by lack of opportunity. When he left home at the age of fourteen, he could barely read and write.

His dream was to get an education.

I'll never know all it took for him to overcome his educational liabilities, but eventually he managed to graduate from Nyack Seminary in preparation for the ministry. When my Phi Beta Kappa mother met him there, she was touched by his love of learning. They were married, and she eagerly began to help him fill the deficits in his educational background. I came along a year later.

As I was growing up I did not feel overt pressure to perform, but I was aware of my father's keen interest in my academic pursuits. He beamed over my straight-A report cards but expressed concern over my lack of mathematical prowess. The message I internalized was that my mother was brilliant in everything, including math, and there I was, the product of their union, perhaps not performing up to the level of the hoped-for DNA that would produce a child with no intellectual deficits.

These thoughts were never expressed to me. I undoubtedly took on more than I was meant to, but I wanted my father to feel gratified by my ability to perform academically. Meanwhile, he never fully understood my pleasure in being the pitcher for the girls softball team of Battleground Junior High and how gratifying it was to pitch a winning game over first-ranked Camus Junior High. Neither did he understand my excitement at being on the Battleground High School tennis team. Neither of my parents were athletically inclined; in contrast, I loved all sports and wanted to be on every team that would have me. I glowed when Miss Safred told my mother I was every PE teacher's dream.

Dad lived long enough to see me complete my first master's degree. That thrilled him. My first book was published shortly after his death, and that too would have thrilled him. That I've completed a second master's degree and written eight books since his death would undoubtedly have made up for my math deficit. My mother would also have been pleased with me—but she was always pleased with me. I was not making up for her deficits or living out her unrealized dreams.

Dream Yearnings

Do I resent the unexpressed dreams and expectations my father placed on me? I don't think so. I am living in an arena of inherent strength, and there is great pleasure that comes with that. What I mean when I say "inherent strength" is that teaching, counseling, and speaking are in my skill set. I can do that. Running an accounting firm, working as a bank teller, or processing mortgage loans is not in my skill set. If I were to try those jobs, the businesses would fail, and I'd be unemployed! With or without my desire to fulfill my father's unmet dreams, I cannot imagine doing anything other than what I'm doing. There is also spiritual assurance that God's plan is being lived out in my life, which produces great peace. Besides, I was never good enough in tennis to consider that as a career anyway.

God knows what He's doing when He places His desire in our heart to do what He has ordained for us from the beginning of time. My dad's wishes were incidental to God's plan, but

Dad's wishes were used by God for the accomplishment of His divine plan. There's something very comforting about all that; everyone wins.

People's experience with personal dreams is as varied as the people themselves. No one's dream history is the same as another's, and yet we all know what it is to have dream yearnings. I think the very existence of those yearnings ties into God's personal dreams for our lives. He placed within us an awareness of certain preferences and in the awareness of those preferences we can find our dreams and motivations. In other words, He places the dreams, and we live them out. When we do, there is internal peace.

Yesterday while Patsy Clairmont and I were at the Dallas airport baggage claim, waiting for our luggage to come bursting through the chute, I asked her if her dreams for her life had been realized. She looked quizzically at me, commended me for such deep ponderings after completing a busy conference weekend, but answered my question with an equally ponderous couple of statements. She said, "My dreams died at a very early age. They died almost as soon as they were born. But ultimately, they were reborn; and surprisingly, they are being lived out, even as I stand here waiting for my luggage."

I was so captivated by her statements I missed seeing and then grabbing my bag; it headed around the corner for a rerun. She waited with me and asked why I had inquired about her dreams. I explained that I was writing a chapter on personal dreams and was wondering about her dreams and the degree to which they were lived out in her life. We talked more. I think you might like to hear what she said about her dreams. I asked if I could simply quote her thoughts, which she sent to me later in the day. Here's what she said:

My dreams died young, and by the time I was in my twenties I was housebound with fear. I had low expectations for my life, so the good things that eventually unfolded for me were all more than I could have believed or even dreamed for my life.

As a little girl I wanted to be a dancer and a writer. I took ballet lessons, and one day the teacher contacted my mother because she thought I showed unusual potential for my age and she wanted permission to work with me individually. My mom had just experienced a spiritual awakening and had joined a highly conservative church that scowled at dancing. So she not only didn't let me have the individual lessons but she pulled me from my dance class. Mom did what she felt was best for me, and it may have been, but it was a hard jolt to my little twirling heart.

I have loved words since birth. I'm almost certain I came out jabbering—probably on the need for speed-limit signs in the birth canal (I tend to be a crusader). As a youngster I wanted to write for a newspaper, and I had told my best friend who was a wanna-be artist that we would one day do books together. But my life took a sharp turn down a windy path when I quit school and the following year married at the ripe old age of seventeen.

By the time I was housebound [with agoraphobia], I had no dreams. Fear had snuffed them out. I was too busy just trying to survive my panic attacks. Besides, I had no education and zero self-esteem. My big prayer was, "Lord give me the courage to get to the grocery store and back home again." That was as far as my mind could stretch for my future.

It would be years before I would risk dreaming for anything. And when it happened, that fluttery feeling in one's heart when a dream begins to form rose up unexpectedly . . .

I was at a women's one-day retreat standing in the back of the room by an exit in case I wanted to flee to the safety of my home a mile away. A lady approached the stage to give book reviews, and as she read a few lines from one of the books laughter from the audience wafted into the air and my heart leapt and my pulse fluttered. I thought, *I want to do that. I want to talk about books and make people laugh.*

I had no idea that God was stirring up the ashes of my buried dreams. They had died in me so many years before that I couldn't imagine I would get to "dance" across various stages proclaiming His liberty to others, nor that my speaking would open the doors for me to write.

If you, like I, have had the privilege of reading Patsy's books or hearing her speak, you will marvel that her dream has not always been alive. And yet it is perhaps her dream's "late stirring" that has been an encouragement to thousands of others who've never dared to believe in the rebirth of their dreams. Her life is an illustration of a God whose timing and style are utterly unique and consistently trustworthy. She is also an illustration of one whose dreams were so carefully and divinely placed, they could not die; they were meant to be resurrected.

Sometimes the realization of our dreams also has a downside. Sometimes the dream comes true . . . but it comes with a high price. In such cases it might be impossible to imagine that God could take a dream that initially broke a mother's heart and change it into an illustration of His gentle love and tender drama. But since it's impossible to *imagine*, let me tell you how it *happened*. Let me tell you about Lisa Smith and her darling mother Vicki Smith.

Vicki had three miscarriages prior to Lisa'a birth, so when Lisa arrived Vicki was thrilled. But she found it odd that the nurses didn't talk about baby Lisa the way they talked to the other new mothers about their babies. She was also confused by her doctor's inquiry about whether or not Vicki wanted to take Lisa home from the hospital. She thought, *What on earth is he thinking?* Of course she planned to take Lisa home; in fact, Vicki said she would not leave the hospital without Lisa!

A week later, when Vicki took Lisa in to see her doctor, he hesitatingly said, "I'm so sorry to tell you this, Mrs. Smith, but

Lisa shows some signs of Down syndrome. We'll need to do a chromosome test on her when she's four weeks old to confirm it."

During that interminable wait for the diagnosis, Vicki fell more and more in love with her curly-haired baby girl. When the phone call came confirming the Down syndrome diagnosis, Vicki dissolved into a heap of anguished tears. She had been warned she might need to institutionalize Lisa. But there was no way that was an option. Neither was it an option to listen to the advice about not getting too attached or avoiding making Lisa "special" because the little girl's future was uncertain.

Lisa was already special, Vicki thought; that was a given! So Vicki pulled herself together and determined Lisa would be deeply loved and highly regarded in spite of her disability.

Vicki began to educate herself about Down syndrome, and she learned how to help Lisa compensate for the challenges to her physical development. At two months of age Lisa was coached in pulling up and doing other exercises to strengthen her muscle tone. When Lisa was a little older, Vicki found a program that further assisted her in physical and occupational therapy.

The best developmental coaching Lisa got, however, came from her baby sister Lori, who became Lisa's role model and playmate. Lisa learned to mimic and follow Lori, and as a result, continued to steadily grow in her development. Whatever Lori did, Lisa did—or at least tried to do. Lori's sisterly loyalty and unconditional love have been huge contributors to Lisa's development as a now-functioning adult.

Lisa showed a love of music as well as a love for Jesus early in her life. As she sang loudly in church, lost in a spirit of exuberant and innocent expressions of the words of the music, Vicki noticed Lisa attempting some kind of sign language as she sang. She decided to find someone who might actually teach Lisa how to sign.

They asked a woman named Marla who was the high school sign language teacher in their city if she would consider teaching Lisa. Marla agreed and suggested Lisa choose three songs she'd like to learn. Lisa picked three songs from the recordings of well-known professional musician Sandi Patty. Marla taught Lisa how to sign just one of the choruses by showing Lisa how to write out the words of the song then look up the sign in the *American Sign Language Book.* Marla told her to practice the chorus for two weeks. Lisa learned it in two days.

When Vicki took Lisa back to Marla for the next lesson, tears streamed down Marla's face as she watched Lisa sign the entire song. She said never had anyone in her classes learned to sign so quickly and so accurately. Most of her challenged students took more than a year to learn a single song. "Lisa has a gift," Marla said.

Lisa went on to teach herself more than 125 songs, most of which are Sandi Patty's. Ultimately, Lisa was asked to sign one Sunday at her church. There were three morning services, each with around fifteen hundred persons attending. As Lisa signed and worshiped with great abandon, the congregations leaped to their feet in thunderous applause. They saw Jesus's touch upon Lisa's life in spite of the challenge of Down syndrome.

Lisa continued to perfect her understanding of sign language and how to connect each sign with each word. One day she confessed to her mother a very big dream. She wanted to do more than just sign from Sandi's CDs. She dreamed of signing with Sandi Patty in person. She wanted to stand next to her on a stage and perform "In Heaven's Eyes" together under the spotlights.

A lump formed in Vicki's throat. "Oh, honey," she said. "That's a very big dream. Sandi is a famous singer who has sung all over the world. It's hard to imagine that your dream could come true, but let's just pray about it and see what God may do."

In December 2004, Sandi came to Lisa's hometown of Denton, Texas, to do a concert. As Sandi sang, she noticed Lisa in the second row, signing every note. She also noticed Lisa's sweet face of genuine worship as the music wafted through the auditorium, lifting everyone into a spirit of praise. Halfway through the concert, Sandi motioned directly to Lisa to come on stage and do two songs with her.

Now Lisa signs frequently with Sandi Patty. She also has participated in the worship singing at Women of Faith conferences nearly thirty times since 2005. She not only signs with Sandi but also with Larnelle Harris, Kathy Troccoli, Avalon, Sheila Walsh, and BeBe Winans. God has chosen her to illustrate the truth of Lisa's favorite song's message: there are no losers in the eyes of God.

Not only are there no losers in God's creation, there are no surprises to God about His creation. God was not playing catch-up to figure out how something good could come from Lisa's challenges. He knew before the foundation of the world about Lisa and placed within her His dream for her life: that she would love Him, serve Him, honor Him, and reflect His unending creativity as He placed her on platforms all over the country. Lisa is not only living out her dream, she is loving God's.

That's the interesting thing about dreams. They first come from the mind and heart of God, who then places them in the mind and heart of us, His creation. They are bound to our lives by inseparable bonds; God gives our hearts a craving for the dreams He has for us. We don't think up these dreams first; God does. Philippians 2:13 states that truth clearly: "For God is working in you, giving you the desire and the power to do what pleases him."

We live our lives in response to Him. He first gives us the desire of the dream, then He empowers us to do it. That pleases Him. That's the order of things. When God is pleased, I am pleased; when we both are pleased, I experience peace about the dream.

GOD'S DREAM WILL PREVAIL

But what happens when we're not obedient to God's original dream for our lives? What happens when we choose a direction other than the one that fulfills God's dream—when we abandon the dream and try to comfort ourselves in pursuit of something else? Does that mean God also abandons His dream for us?

The question reminds me of the old quip about how to make

God laugh: tell Him your plans. One of my favorite things about God is that He is stronger than I am, smarter than I am, and cares more about everything and everyone than I do. That means nothing, including my misguided determination to follow my own plans or my willful disobedience to do His will, is going to derail God's plan. If you needed to be reminded of that fact, take a second to remember these powerhouse statements from God's Word:

I know, LORD, that a person's life is not his own. No one is able to plan his own course. (Jeremiah 10:23)

You can make many plans, but the LORD's purpose will prevail. (Proverbs 19:21)

Pretty emphatic, aren't they? I suggest to you that swaddled in the word *plan* is the word *dream.* So we could then read that last verse as saying that we may have many dreams but *God's* dream will win out. That is comforting to the one who has abandoned God's dream for her life, and it's inspiring to the one who fears that disobedience, indifference, or spiritual rebellion has stopped God's dream for her life dead in its tracks, never to rise again.

It *will* rise again because God will always prevail.

There again is the mystery of God: He does allow us to do stupid things, but just as the good shepherd goes after one lost sheep, God goes after us. He has a dream for our lives; that dream will prevail because He does.

It's not too late, dear one. If you're not following God's plan for your life, change course! If you've abandoned your dream, reclaim it. God is in the business of turning ashes into beauty. Bring Him your ashes, and then get on with living His dream and yours.

twelve

※

DON'T ABANDON THE REASON YOU WERE BORN

*You are the ones chosen by God, . . . God's instruments
to do his work and speak out for him, to tell others
of the night-and-day difference he made for you.*

1 PETER 2:9 MSG

Since the beginning of time, humankind has puzzled over and considered the questions, *Why was I born? Why am I here? What is the purpose of life?*

The writer of the Old Testament book of Ecclesiastes began his quandary about meaning and purpose in life by saying simply, "Everything is meaningless . . . utterly meaningless!" As if he needed to support his depressing conclusion about life and his participation in it, he added the following commentary:

What do people get for all their hard work? Generations come and go, but nothing really changes. The sun rises and sets and hurries around to rise again. The wind blows south and north, here and there, twisting back and forth, getting nowhere. The rivers run into the sea, but the sea is never full. Then the water returns again to the rivers and flows again to the sea. Everything is so weary and tiresome! No matter how much we see, we are never satisfied. No matter how much we hear, we are not content. (Ecclesiastes 1:3–8)

When things go wrong, pessimism comes naturally. It's not unusual to hear those in the middle of emotional depression, personal heartache, financial calamity, or social disaster pondering whether their lives are meaningless and futile. Hardship can make us question whether our lives are actually serving a purpose. Lost in despair, we may, perhaps without really meaning to, drift—or plunge—into an emotional and spiritual void.

In this final chapter, I hope I can help you recognize your true reason for living so that, no matter what events come your way, you never abandon the purpose for which you were created.

THE PROFOUNDLY SIMPLE ANSWER TO "WHY WAS I BORN?"

A short time ago, my nine-year-old grandson Alec experienced his own version of the question "Why was I born, and what's the point anyway?" He and my daughter Beth were driving to the grocery store one afternoon, and Alec just cut loose with a barrage of hurt and resentment over how he was being treated by his big brother, Ian. According to Alec, Ian did nothing but pick fights, refuse to say "Hi" to him at school, talk mean to him, and take his iPod without permission. No amount of conversation would convince Alec that he was not an innocent victim at the hands of an unreasonable and tyrannical brother.

Tentatively, Beth asked Alec if he had considered praying about the relationship with Ian. In yet another barrage of words, Alec said, "Mom, I became a Christian three years ago, I got baptized, and I tithe my allowance; what more am I supposed to do? Besides, Ian would be mean to me whether I prayed or not, and that's something I know for sure! But here's something I *don't* know for sure: Why was I even born? Everything is too hard."

Several days later, Alec scored the winning point for his basketball team, sending them to the tournament's semifinals to be played the following week. Pandemonium broke out on the court as Alec was raised to the less-than-sturdy shoulders of his nine-year-old teammates and declared the hero of the entire season! On the ride home, Alec could not contain himself he was so filled with self-congratulatory praise. In the midst of it all, he announced, "Now I know why I was born. I was born to be a victory leader. How cool is that?"

Ian's muttered "Yeah, Alec, that's cool" barely registered on the Richter scale.

Many of us assume, like Alec, that we were born to do something great, perhaps something that would change the world and make it a better place. We look at people like Oprah Winfrey, who recently founded the forty-million-dollar Oprah Winfrey Leadership Academy for disadvantaged girls in South Africa. She has also built sixty schools in thirty countries through her Angel Network and donated more than two hundred million dollars to educational and children's organizations around the world. As the ribbon was cut inaugurating her South African school, she was quoted as saying, "I was born for this!"

Others share Oprah's generous desire to meet the needs of others. Rock star Bono has an equally impressive zeal to educate as well as to bring medical attention to needy children around the world. With these sterling examples of greatness and generosity, we could shrink back into our relatively uneventful lives and feel ashamed that we have contributed no particular greatness for the betterment of the world. Instead, we wake up each morning, eat our Ezekiel toast and sip our green tea that tastes like lawn clippings, and go on with our day. We go to bed at night, with or without Ambien, wake up, and start all over again. Few of us would exult over this routine and crow, "I was born for this!"

But we need to take a minute and ask the question, "Why was I born?" in light of Scripture. Does it answer that weighty question? The answer is yes. In fact, it answers the question with profound simplicity.

Refresh your memory with Ephesians 1:4, which states, "Long ago, even before he made the world, God loved us." This amazing scripture says He loved us before He flung the stars into place or created the coastline of Laguna Beach, California. We got top love-billing before absolutely every other created thing. He loved us even before He created us. Does that not blow your mind?

We find the same theme in Ephesians 1:11, which states, "He chose us from the beginning, and all things happen just as he decided long ago." What was it He chose? He chose to create us so that He might love us. He chose us to be the recipients of His never-ending, unfathomable love.

So then, why were we born? *We were born to be loved by God!* Plain and simple!

And just in case you wonder how you can actually believe you rank higher in His divine heart than, say, Laguna Beach, California, read this verse from James 1:18: "And we, out of all creation, became his choice possession." We are it! God's best and His most loved! We don't even have to go to the playoffs. We've already won! We were born for that!

Some of you may be muttering a bit. I can hear you saying, "How can you reduce that huge question about why we were born to such a simplistic 'God created us so He could love us' answer?" I didn't reduce it; God did. The reason that simple answer seems too simple is because we have such an "I've got to *earn* love" mentality. That mentality says we can't just sit back and enjoy God's preference for us over anything in the world. We have to do something to qualify for that love.

Ken and I did not have children so they could help around the house. We had children for the express purpose of loving them and having a relationship with them. By the same token,

God did not create us to help around the earth. He did not create us to do what He can already do. He created us so that He might love us and have a relationship with us. Then, based on His love, we return that love, thus establishing a reciprocal relationship. We need to understand that we don't have to do anything to earn this relationship. God ordained it "even before he made the world."

PARTNERING WITH GOD IN HIS DREAM FOR US

One night after dinner, our seven-year-old Jeff announced that he'd decided he would always do the dishes for me. In fact, he solemnly swore he would do the dishes for me every day until he was sixteen. I was touched by his generosity but curious about the cutoff time of age sixteen. I thanked him but asked what happens at age sixteen. He said he would be married by then and would do his wife's dishes. Apparently when that event occurred I'd be on my own.

Now, why did Jeff offer to do my dishes? Was he trying to earn the right to a bed, dinner, and Tonka trucks? No. He made his offer out of his love for me. His love prompted him to do something for me. That's the way love works. We respond to love by giving back in love, but giving back is the *second* step. The first step is *receiving* love.

Jeff was receiving love from his father and me. He wanted to give love back. His way of giving back and showing appreciation was to do something. That is the same principle we use with our service to God. He loves me. I love Him back. I love Him back by doing something for Him. What do I do for Him that shows my love? I read His Book that expresses His love as well as instructs me how to live my life in ways that will please Him. Because all relationships thrive on communication, I talk to Him. I have regular prayer times when I express my love for Him and seek His wisdom for everything I am doing or even thinking of doing. We have a reciprocal relationship. He gives, and I give.

I think one of the most gracious ways God receives our love is to make us partners with Him. We become partners with Him in doing those things that make the world a better place. We already know God could get things done without us, but He wants us to be a part of everything He does. That's where the divine placement of dreams or plans comes into being. God places them within us as motivators to accomplish His already conceived dream plan. So we do together what He could do alone because working in isolation is not His preference.

When Jesus established His earthly ministry, He chose twelve disciples to partner with Him. They not only had a relationship with Jesus, they ultimately spread the news that He was the Son of God. When they didn't understand His miracles, Jesus explained them. When they didn't get the meaning of His parables, Jesus taught them. He also taught them how to love and how to live in the divine reciprocity of give-and-take. All that teaching from Jesus helped them later to establish the Christian church after the resurrection of Jesus and His return to heaven.

God's concept of partnering is a tremendous relief to us because we realize it is not we who are fully responsible for the results of our efforts to serve. Ephesians 3:20 reminds us we depend on His power within us to accomplish His dream: "By his mighty power at work within us, he is able to accomplish infinitely more than we would ever dare to ask or hope." Our internal engine is powered by Him—not just by ourselves. We serve and work together.

Not only do we return God's love through a personal relationship of prayer and Bible study, we also love Him by loving His creation. Repeatedly Scripture tells us we are to love one another. That loving of others is our agreement that all God's creation is worthy of our love as well as His. That's another area of partnering. (I know . . . I hear you muttering that not *all* of God's creation is lovable, but that's another matter. Maybe we'll deal with that in some other publication. I know I need to "chat" regularly with myself about that!)

COMMUNICATING GOD'S LOVE TO HIS CREATION

Jesus told the disciples to "go into all the world and preach the gospel" (Mark 16:15 NKJV). That message is for us as well. We are to spread the good news that Jesus is the Son of God and that through Him we find forgiveness of sin and the hope of eternal life. The "go into all the world" is a literal command. In fact, when we don't go into those places in the world where the needs of God's creation are not being met, it hurts the heart of God. Isaiah 59:16 states, "He was amazed to see that no one intervened to help the oppressed."

When we help the oppressed we are communicating God's love message to His creation. What is that message? Isaiah 63:7 states, "I will tell of the LORD's unfailing love."

World Vision is an organization that has been partnering with God in bringing the good news of God's love all over the world. They are especially involved with bringing aid and encouragement to the world's oppressed and quite specifically to the children of those oppressed. Bob Pierce, the organization's founder, said, "Let my heart be broken by the things that break the heart of God."

In December 2006, I went to Africa with other members of the Women of Faith organization to visit a new World Vision project for the Kipsigis people of southwest Kenya. Poor roads with potholes big enough for a baby elephant help make this one of the most remote and inaccessible districts of Kenya. The impoverished people of this area have not been able to receive government services like education and health care that are more readily available in other parts of the country. Only recently has this little population and its needs become known to those who are responding to the call to help the oppressed.

In 2005 World Vision established what is called the Kirindon Area Development Project for those people. They identified a woman named Rebecca as one in critical need of help. We all piled into three Land Rovers and began the bone-jarring five-hour trip through the Massai Mara animal preserve, with its roaming zebras, elephants, and giraffes that stared at us with mild curiosity, as we made our way to Rebecca's little village. There we saw for ourselves that which breaks the heart of God.

When we arrived we were led into Rebecca's windowless hut with its dirt floors and mud walls. Rebecca told us her story in Swahili, which was translated by a World Vision staff person. We were spellbound and heartbroken as we learned her two daughters are buried in unmarked graves behind her hut. Both died of AIDS, leaving children for Rebecca to care for.

One day Rebecca's husband simply walked away, leaving her without any means of support. She had six children to feed, five of them under age nine. She worked in other people's fields for a few shillings to provide food, but it was never enough. "We begged the neighbors for food but still had only one meal a day. The children were malnourished. I was so discouraged. In desperation I thought about giving one of my children away to be a laborer for a neighbor in exchange for food."

At the point of her greatest need, the World Vision Kirindon Project selected Immanuel, Rebecca's nine-year-old grandson, to be a part of the child-sponsorship program. That meant Rebecca's family immediately received two months' worth of protein-rich beans along with peas and cooking oil. They also received twenty pounds of seed corn. That explained the neat rows of corn we saw growing behind her hut.

This assistance helped save Rebecca's children from malnourishment and helped her start a business selling vegetables at the community shopping center. With the little profit she saves, she wants to qualify for a small business loan through World Vision that will help her expand her vegetable business.

As we stood in a circle in Rebecca's hut, we were especially touched as Immanuel asked us if we would like to see his "other family." He carefully removed from his pocket a picture of nine-year-old twin boys from Minnesota. Because those little boys had selected Immanuel as their sponsored child, their monthly support enabled Immanuel and his family to survive. The picture showed two blond smiling little boys whom Immanuel claims as his brothers. Rebecca told us he carries the picture with him wherever he goes.

Rebecca also told us the World Vision people made it clear they were not the answer to her problems in life; God is. She had never thought about God, but she and the children are now going to a little village church. She is learning there is a God who sees her, loves her, and promises to never leave her. As she told this part of her story, she threw her head back, clapped her hands together, and laughed. "I'm not afraid anymore. See, He is taking care of me. He is taking care of my children. He loves us. That is the most wonderful thing I ever knew."

I must admit, it was one of the most wonderful experiences I've ever witnessed. To see this dear woman come to an understanding of how fully she is loved and cared for brought tears to the eyes of all of us.

We spent several more hours there outside Rebecca's hut mingling with scores of children and adults who came streaming in from who knows where. We had brought gifts of paper, pencils, crayons, twirling tops, candy, and chewing gum, all of which were received with waves of enthusiasm. We sat on benches brought in for the occasion and sang songs together. They had learned some Christian hymns from their little church, so they sang in Swahili and we in English. Soon the little crowd of people grew even larger, and everyone began to dance to tambourines and a drum. It was a phenomenal expression of gratitude and joy from people who were learning the heart of God had been broken for them and that their broken pieces were being put together again by Him as well as those with whom He partners.

This past weekend I was presenting the World Vision project to the eighteen thousand women at a Women of Faith conference in Columbus, Ohio. Alec and Ian were sitting in the front row along with their mother, Beth. When the faces of Rebecca, Immanuel, and the other children flashed on the monitor screens, the story took on greater meaning for my grandsons. They sat in rapt attention as I explained that child sponsorship could be a matter of life and death.

At the break following the presentation, Beth and the boys dashed to the World Vision table and picked their way through hundreds of individual folders containing the life stories and pictures of children available for sponsorship. They settled on the folder picturing a little boy named Jeffrey from Kenya. They chose him because their uncle is named Jeff and he, like the child, has a February birthday.

They were so excited over their selection. Alec said to me,

"My very own sponsored child has a chance at life now." At lunchtime when he and I were chatting, I asked if he remembered telling his mom he didn't know why he was born. He remembered but didn't know why I brought it up. I said to him, "Alec, sponsoring that little Jeffrey from Kenya is one of the many reasons you were born. You were born to love God and to share His love with others. You are doing that very thing when your allowance helps Jeffrey to realize he is loved by someone in America and he is loved by the God of heaven."

Of course Ian couldn't resist asking Alec if that was better than being the "victory leader" in basketball.

I was tempted to quickly change the subject to avoid conflict, but Alec quickly answered, "No, Ian, this sponsored-kid thing is better."

God's Profound Love Principle at Work

Let's circle back to the way we started this chapter and think once again on the question of why we were born. If we conclude that life is meaningless, as the Ecclesiastes writer suggested at the beginning of his book, we don't need to bother figuring out an answer to why we were born. It wouldn't matter one way or the other. If, however, we respond to the fact of God loving us as the reason we were born, the sky's the limit in how we conduct our lives. God's love gives us purpose; it gives us a great depth of meaning. We then partner with Him as we experience that meaning and how it is to be communicated.

Most of us can't contribute millions of dollars or go out into the far corners of the world to help the oppressed and communicate God's love. My grandsons are learning they can help the oppressed and never leave their home in Ohio. That realization has broadened their understanding of how to be a partner with God. As Alec said to me before he left for home that weekend in Columbus, "I'm savin' a kid's life, Maungya, and did you tell me that's why I was born?"

"Responding to God loving you and then sharing it with others is the deal, Alec," I told him. "That's why you were born." For some reason my words produced a look of slight boredom on his face, but he hugged me anyway. Maybe I used too many words.

The Bob Pierce statement, "Let my heart be broken by the things that break the heart of God," lingers in my mind as I conclude this chapter . . . and the book. I hope you see the profound love principle at work that prompted God to create you. Psalm 139 describes how carefully He watches over the processes that knit you together in your mother's womb. We are not mass produced. We are one-of-a-kind creations over whom God always has a loving and watchful eye. He calls us by name. He knows how many hairs are on our heads; He knows when we stand up and when we sit down. He is never indifferent to any hurt, challenge, or joy we experience in life. His ear is ever inclined toward our voice when we call out to Him.

And yet, how easily and frequently we can break the heart of God by not responding to His offer of love for each one of us personally designed, one-of-a-kind creations. The most poignant image of breaking the heart of God is provided for us as we read the words of Jesus looking out over the city of Jerusalem:

> O Jerusalem, Jerusalem, the city that kills the prophets and stones God's messengers! How often I have wanted to gather your children together as a hen protects her chicks beneath her wings, but you wouldn't let me. (Matthew 23:37)

We have all had our hearts broken by someone who did not choose us, or by someone who rejected our offer of love that would have brought the fulfillment of a relationship. Some of us have even said under our breath, "It's your loss. I would have been good for you. We could have had a great life together, but . . . oh, well."

God never says, "Oh, well." He is relentless in His love pursuit of us while at the same time honoring our right to say, "No, I'm not interested." But just as Jesus's heart was broken as He said to Jerusalem, "You wouldn't let me," so it breaks the heart of God when we don't let Him fulfill His desires for us.

Let me say yet again: meaning for life comes when we realize God made us because He wanted to. First John 4:10 states, "It is not that we loved God, but that he loved us." God made the first move; we choose whether to make the next one. It is a sobering freedom to abandon the love God has for us. In so doing we abandon the very reason we were born, and our lives then are reduced to a meaningless existence.

GOD LOVES US, NEVER LEAVES US

Throughout this book, we've discussed the inseparable bonds our hearts crave, and we've explored what happens when those bonds are damaged through abandonment, remembering that *abandon* means "to choose against; to desert." How blessed we are that, in the cocooning security of God's choice to love us, we also have His promise to *never* abandon us. He will not desert us; He will never choose against us. No human being in our lives can make such a declaration of steadfast love. Only God can; only God does. Let's remember yet again Isaiah 41:9, which promises us, "I have chosen you and will not throw you away."

My prayer for you is that you choose to accept the very reason for which you were born and that you rest in your place of one whom God will never abandon . . . never throw away.

Notes

one The Look—and Feel—of Abandonment

    1. Dr. Evelyn Bassoff, *Mothers and Daughters* (New York: New American Library, 1988), 23.

two Tracking Tracers Back to Their Root

    1. Alice Miller, *Thou Shalt Not Be Aware* (New York: American Library, 1986), 47.

    2. Ibid., 47.

    3. Judith Viorst, *Necessary Losses* (New York: Ballantine, 1987), 22.

WOMEN OF FAITH®

Women of Faith, North America's largest women's conference, is an experience like no other. Thousands of women — all ages, sizes, and backgrounds — come together in arenas for a weekend of love and laughter, stories and encouragement, drama, music, and more. The message is simple. The result is life-changing.

What this conference did for me was to show me how to celebrate being a woman, mother, daughter, grandmother, sister or friend.
— Anne, Corona, CA

I appreciate how genuine each speaker was and that they were open and honest about stories in their life   even the difficult ones.
— Amy, Fort Worth, TX

GO, you MUST go. The Women of Faith team is wonderful, uplifting, funny, blessed. Don t miss out on a chance to have your life changed by this incredible experience.
— Susan, Hartford, CT